"Friends are those rare people who ask how we are and then wait to hear the answer"

Ed Cunningham

The Friendship Book

A THOUGHT FOR EACH DAY | 2021

January

RICHARD JEFFERIES, the son of a Wiltshire farmer, ran away from home twice in search of adventure.

First, he aimed for Paris, then America, but he ended up back on the home farm both times.

He began scribbling and made a name for himself as a nature writer.

Indeed, his communion with the natural world was regarded by some as mystical, which suggests to me only that he paid closer attention to its wonders than most of us do.

Writing of woods in Sussex in January 1884, he said, "The lost leaves measure our years; they are gone as the days are gone, and the bare branches silently speak of a new year, slowly advancing its buds, its foliage, and fruit."

The year 1884 seems like such a long time away, but not much will have changed in the woods, and our lives still have their seasons. The supposedly empty times are not forsaken; they are necessary in as much as they clear the way for the new.

May this new year, in whichever way you need it the most, also be full of new buds, foliage and fruit.

JANUARY is thought to be named after the Roman god Janus. He, so the myth says, had the ability to look backwards and forwards simultaneously.

But he was also the god of the beginnings and the ends of conflicts.

Perhaps our resolutions for the year ahead could focus on ending conflicts that may have started in the last 12 months.

A year with less conflict and more harmony in it – that has to be something well worth looking forward to.

WHEN your days are filled with problems
And you don't know what to do,
Life turns up surprises
When you least expect it to.

A chance word from a stranger,
A letter from a friend,
A glowing sky at sunset –
God's blessings never end.

Then to your weary heart there comes
A tiny little spark
Of hope, to bring you shining through
And lift you from the dark.

Marian Cleworth

WE live in a disposable world these days, with so many things used once and thrown away. We drink from a plastic bottle, then disregard the bottle.

Generally, it is seen as a bad thing.

But there's another take on a disposable world.

Has a stranger ever done a good turn for you and said something like "Think nothing of it"? Have you ever done the same?

Has anyone ever slowed to let you past, or held a door open for you, then carried on with their day? Some people positively litter their path with goodness.

I wouldn't like to guess how many kind or courteous deeds are used every day – used once and then thought no more about.

The difference is, of course, that such deeds don't harm the planet; they help the people living on it.

They can be easily recycled, with one kindness almost inevitably creating another like it.

And they come from an infinitely renewable source – love!

That's the kind of single-use, disposable world we could all live happily in.

A letter on the mat can bring good news.

9

ON days when I have been indoors too long, I put my boots on and start walking. The first mile is through town.

Where the dirt path approaches the hill, I start to feel at peace. Yet tracks in the grass assure me I am not alone. The breeze on my cheeks encourages me to pay attention. The puddles I encounter encourage my inner child.

Rising, the hill offers ever-changing points of view and the time to properly consider them. The farther I get from my own four walls, the more I feel at home in something larger.

I need only take a step – slightly forwards and slightly upwards – to achieve something. And other worries become a little farther away.

The view from the summit fills my heart with hope and a sense that, despite all the things I am not doing, I have done something simple but profound.

The path home sees me revitalised, ready for the tasks of the day.

Can you see why I think of this hill as a friend?

DID you ever have a three-dimensional picture when you were younger, Francis?"

Nothing Mary says surprises me these days, but wondering at her point, I did permit myself a quizzical expression.

"You remember," she encouraged. "They had flat card on one side and ridged plastic on the other. The picture under the plastic side would look mundane and slightly out of focus at first glance."

"Yes," I agreed. "And if you looked at it just right, it suddenly had depth and things seemed to reach out to you!"

Well, I had stumbled on to the answer she was hoping for all along.

"Just like life, don't you think?"

And off she walked. Smiling.

Perhaps I should focus more on my dear friend Mary and not walking into the philosophical traps (or lessons) she keeps laying in my way!

Of course, I never will.

Thursday — January 7

H E'S been driving as long as me," Harry said. "Mostly on the same roads. But he says they're full of chancers and crazy people."

"What do you think?" I asked.

"Haven't you been watching?" he asked.

He drove on in silence, focusing, I thought, on manoeuvring around a winding road with plenty of parked cars on either side.

Then I saw the little waves.

Harry would raise a hand slightly, acknowledging another driver slowing down to let him past.

Yet another driver, appreciating being let out of a driveway, would do the same to him.

"How many of those have there been?" I asked.

"In the past three or four minutes? About eight."

Bad drivers, like bad people, make a big noise, while courteous drivers and kind people go on quietly doing what they do. There are many more of the latter, of course.

It's just that we see what we look for. Harry looks for the little waves.

Friday — January 8

I HESITATE to say it, because it seems to take away from the purity of the thing. But I have often thought that the best thing a person can do for themselves is to be generous to others.

Why?

Because, in ways too difficult to predict – ways that almost suggest a higher influence – the person who gives generally receives more.

Thus generosity, against all expectation, almost becomes a selfish thing!

I was reminded of this when reading these words accredited to the Chinese philosopher Confucius:

"The benevolent man is attracted to benevolence because he feels at home in it. The wise man is attracted to benevolence because he finds it to his advantage."

So, it seems, despite what some cynics might suggest, that it is possible to be both wise and benevolent.

11

Saturday — January 9

DO you have faith? I don't mean "Do you have religion?" People who have never set foot in a place of worship might still have faith, even if they aren't sure what in. In times when they have no resources left, they will still hang on in the hope that something will see them through.

They might refer to that something as luck or blind chance, but a part of them knows there is something more. And it's there for us.

The Indian poet Rabindranath Tagore described it this way: "Faith is the bird that feels the light and sings when the dawn is still dark."

Feel it. Sing!

Sunday — January 10

I KNOW people who need to have things just right. Their drive for perfection can sometimes take a heavy emotional toll.

In Muslim countries and Amish communities in the United States, rug-weavers and quilt-makers deliberately put imperfections into their finished products. Why?

Because, despite being of different faiths, both believe only God is perfect, and it is foolish for humans to aspire to be like that aspect of him.

Relax a little. We all make mistakes. I have never seen perfection, but I doubt that much grows from it. By its very definition, perfection is a dead-end.

I have, however, seen God make many beautiful and wonderful things happen as the result of some very human mistakes.

Monday — January 11

AT this time of year, most of us will be up in time to see the sun rise.

Henry David Thoreau wrote in his book, "Walden", "It is true I have never materially assisted the sun in his rising, but, doubt not, it was of the last importance only to be present at it."

The wonders of the world we cannot assist, we can – and it is no small thing – still appreciate.

A spectacular sunrise.

Kent's white cliffs.

Tuesday — January 12

THEY say that time heals all things.

I'm not convinced that is true. At best, time can heal, but sometimes it simply makes a wound or a brokenness not matter any more.

Do you know what heals all things? Love. But it's not as simple as that.

There also needs to be the willingness to apply that love. Applying it in extraordinary amounts, in some cases.

If we have the will to keep applying that remedy, then love – intentional love – really will heal all things.

Wednesday — January 13

A PROVERB from the Middle East suggests we "balance each hour given to this world with an hour given to the next."

If you believe in a next world, that would seem very good advice. If you don't, then you might give those hours to the wellbeing of others.

Either way, I imagine the next world will be very happy.

Thursday — January 14

IMAGINE what a nerve-racking job it was to compile the first-ever dictionary of the English language.

Someone was always going to say, "You missed out –", or "It doesn't mean that!"

Indeed, that first dictionary was reworked many times.

With that possibility for failure or criticism in mind, Samuel Johnson might easily have decided not to attempt his great work.

Instead, he wrote in the preface the following: "When it shall be found that much is omitted, let it not be forgotten that much likewise is performed."

Criticism is important, but when we criticise let's not attach too much importance to the mistakes.

Always remember what was intended and the courage it took to stand up and try.

Friday — January 15

W E have fond memories of some strange things," I suggested. "Like huddling under blankets for warmth; scratching pictures in the frost on the inside of a bedroom window; like taking a candle to light the way to bed because there was no electricity."

"Perhaps," my sweetheart said, "because we overcame them."

Hmm. Perhaps, one day, people will look back as fondly on central-heating and double-glazing.

Somehow, I don't think so.

Difficult times in life are never nice to go through, but they do bring something better times don't offer – the chance to overcome!

Saturday — January 16

O N a ferry crossing to Ireland I stumbled and asked a passing crew member, "How long does it take to get your sea legs?"

"It's easy," she replied. "Each step you take, put your foot down until it reaches the deck. No less and no more.

"What causes the problem is putting your foot down where you think the deck ought to be and not where it actually is."

If I'd been feeling a little less green, I might have thought there was a philosophy for life there!

Sunday — January 17

I N the early 1900s, Christian writer Walter de la Mare wrote a children's rhyme about a horse that could run so far and so fast that its rider was always under the noonday sun with a "never-lengthening shadow".

People mocked them, but it mattered not a jot, for the mockers were soon overtaken by the night, while rider and horse were always in the day.

The unstated message being, I think, that if we position ourselves well – under the sun – then we needn't worry overmuch about the reactions of others.

Let them settle wherever they will, while we strive always to be in the light.

THIS world has been well and truly mapped. But do you know where even the most intrepid explorers have never discovered? The Safe Place.

You know, that magical place where we put important things for safe-keeping, only to never see them again.

William Cowper must have had it in mind when he wrote: "For 'tis a truth well known to most, that whatsoever thing is lost:

"We seek it, ere it come to light, in every cranny but the right."

A RAMBLING conversation on a long walk turned to favourite proverbs and sayings.

I told Harry some of my favourites.

He told me some of his.

And we discussed their merits or demerits.

"There's a Turkish proverb I like," I said. "'The man who listens is wiser than the man who talks.'"

To which my friend, although I do wonder why I call him that sometimes, smiled and kept on walking.

NO more than tools of the trade," Jimmy said, dismissing my nonsense.

I had suggested he might have had a special bond with some of the sheepdogs he worked with across the decades.

"If you say so, Jimmy."

My eyes drifted around the room, past photos and paintings of different collies.

There were china ornaments in the shapes of collies, and a worn old leather collar fastened to a wooden plaque.

It wouldn't do for a man who had lived the hard life of an "oot-by hurd", a shepherd of the high hills, to appear soft in his retirement.

Now, would it?

DEAR Lord, I turned the calendar –
Another month gone by!
It looked so fresh and clean and new,
It made me pause and sigh.

What would the weeks ahead all hold
And would I treat them right?
I hoped the days would be all good
And filled with love and light.

Please help me, Lord, to do my best
Whatever lies in store,
Reminding me you're always near
To turn the page once more.

Iris Hesselden

A FLURRY of snow reminded me that such weather would, in certain parts, in times gone by, be called flindrikin.

The word means flouncy, frivolous, insubstantial.

In days with no snow, we would undoubtedly get to work. In days of heavy snow, we would stay huddled inside.

How nice, occasionally, to have a day where it's too snowy for work but not snowy enough to hide. To play in a flindrikin sort of way!

IF only everyone was like me! But if we all thought the same, how boring. The differences between people can be the cause of a lot of dissatisfaction.

The poet Percy Bysshe Shelley thought they might be a good thing.

"We – are we not formed, as notes of music are; for each other, though dissimilar?"

It's not that the differences are intrinsically bad. It might just be that mankind hasn't learned to sing in harmony yet.

But, oh, when it does!

Sunday — January 24

JOSEPH ADDISON was an essayist, playwright and poet who lived at the turn of the 19th century. He had this to say of literary criticism.

"A true critic ought to dwell rather upon excellencies than imperfections, to discover the concealed beauties of a writer, and communicate to the world such things as are worth their observation."

Or, as the Apostle Paul put in his letter to the Philippians:

"Whatever is true, whatever is noble, whatever is right, whatever is pure, whatever is lovely, whatever is admirable – if anything is excellent or praiseworthy – think about such things."

Monday — January 25

ON one of our shelves sits a tin box. What's in it? Buttons. I once asked the Lady of the House why she kept Great-aunt Louisa's button box.

"You look and you see thirty-four different buttons," she explained. "I see thirty-four different ways of holding things together.

"And, bless her heart, with a quiet word, some practical advice, a place to retreat to, even a serious or sorrowful look, Louisa 'buttoned' the family together in more ways than one."

Tuesday — January 26

IT'S my first memory," Harry said, toeing a drift of snow. "I wasn't yet two.

"My mother had opened the front door to show us a blanket of white, level with the bottom of the door. I remember wondering what it would be like to fall forward into that sparkling white stuff."

"And did you?" I asked.

"I don't remember," he replied. "But I do remember that sense of curiosity. It has been a great gift, responsible for many wonderful experiences over the years. And maybe if this snow gets a little deeper . . ."

Curiosity. A gift from whom, I wondered, curious.

THE earth lay hard and cold and still,
The sky was dark and grey;
The wind blew cold and chilled our bones –
A dreary winter's day.
But then a break across the clouds,
And soon the sun appeared.
It quickly lifted hearts and minds
And sadness disappeared.

The wind remained as strong and chill;
The earth still seemed asleep,
But suddenly we felt new hope
The road was not as steep.
A little sunshine gives us joy
Just as a smile can do,
So catch the sunshine when you can
And share a smile or two!

Iris Hesselden

HOPE BOURNE lived for more than 50 years in the wilder parts of Exmoor, living mostly off the land and surviving by her own wits.

She wrote several books and many newspaper articles based on her experiences out on the moor.

Her writing was descriptive and filled with fascinating insights. Her love of the land, its history and the creatures who live there was beyond doubt.

Often, nothing much happened in her stories. She might describe a sunset, or a passing rider, or a sheep somewhere it shouldn't be.

But she made the reader feel they were there and something important was happening. How? By paying attention and appreciating.

Of course, Hope Bourne had the advantage of living in a stunning part of the country. But any place will seem more wonderful if you pay close enough attention, and appreciation makes everything more beautiful. Why not try it where you call home?

Friday — January 29

JOHN values his home comforts, has a few friends, enjoys watching sports. He works as an accountant.

Only once did I hear him wax philosophical. That was when he told me, "It's all about balance."

Oh! As philosophies went that had to be the simplest, perhaps the shallowest, I'd ever heard.

Well, that was several years ago, and you know what? There hasn't been a single situation I have found myself in where John's words didn't apply. Life. It is all about balance.

Saturday — January 30

IN some countries there is a tradition of laying different objects in front of a child and watching which it is attracted to. It's a way – supposedly – of telling the child's future.

If it crawls towards a coin, a future in business beckons; a preference for a writing implement indicates a scholar; whereas reaching for a toy might imply a wasted life.

The friend who told me this said his father had conducted a similar experiment with him.

"Which did you choose?" I asked.

"None of them," he replied. "I crawled over them to get to my father. He didn't realise I saw him – or perhaps being like him – as one of the options."

Business, learning and play are all very fine. But family beats them all.

Sunday — January 31

I OFTEN hear people say, "Oh, that's just the way I am". But we needn't settle for that – we can work on "the way I want to be".

As a young man, at the end of the 1600s, Isaac Watts wrote this:

"I'll not willingly offend,
Nor willingly be offended.
What's amiss I'll strive to mend,
And endure what can't be mended."

The little box that holds a host of memories.

February

Monday — February 1

BUT I am very poorly today and very stupid and hate everybody and everything."

What would you think of the person who said such a thing? Self-pitying? Not very bright? Perhaps unlikely to amount to much?

These words were written by Charles Darwin, naturalist, geologist and biologist. His misery at that time may well have been due to illness caused by a spider bite.

He wrote "On The Origin Of Species" and has had more than 120 species named after him. His eventual passing was commemorated with a tomb in Westminster Abbey.

Why am I saying this?

Perhaps to remind us all not to write someone off just because they are having a bad day. Their best days – and ours, if we are the ones feeling down – may simply not have arrived yet!

Tuesday — February 2

TODAY is Candlemas. That has various meanings in the Christian church. It might refer to the purification of the Virgin Mary, or the presentation of Jesus at the temple for the first time.

Candles are brought to the church to be blessed, the light they give off being compared to Jesus, "the light of the world".

As with many church traditions, there is an older element. The ancient Celts believed that spring, in the form of a maiden, returned to earth from the underworld where she had hidden all winter.

They would celebrate "her" return with offerings. And they would seek blessings upon the candles that had seen them through the winter. That image is a powerful one.

Do you know someone who, just like those candles, gives of themselves to see others through dark times? This Candlemas, why not celebrate them?

Wednesday — February 3

PEOPLE say things like, "When one door closes, somewhere another door opens." It's a nice philosophy, reminding us that there are always other ways to go.

Our dear friend Mary prefers a more pro-active approach.

"When one door closes," she told me, "take it by the handle and open it again. That's how doors work."

Thursday — February 4

I'VE woken to clouds grey and leaden,
My heart plummets down to the floor,
The rain's silver blades pound the pavements
Then swiftly hope springs to the fore.

There's a bright blue line across sea's horizon
Maybe the skies will soon clear?
With luck, then, perhaps we'll see sunshine
And the puddles will fast disappear.

But if the day cannot be as we planned it –
Since the forecast did not mention rain –
We'll seek out some brand-new adventures,
Sometimes a loss turns to gain!

Marian Cleworth

Friday — February 5

MY back was sore and my hands were covered in tile cement. I was weary. Then the co-ordinator of the charity we were fitting the kitchen for stopped at the door.

"Looking really good," he said. "Hopefully, it will outlast us."

"That would be good," I was about to say, "because I don't fancy having to do it again."

But I didn't, because he spoke first.

"It's a blessing to be able to leave the world a little better than we found it."

I thought about that, and my back didn't hurt quite so much.

THE librarian of Canterbury Cathedral in the 11th century issued the monks with a book each for the improvement of their minds and souls.

After a year he would call them together to return the books.

Any monk who had not read the whole book was expected to prostrate himself and explain why in front of everyone.

Suddenly, library late fines don't seem so bad.

Perhaps it might make us appreciate, even more, the importance of a good book.

And how lucky we are to have access to so many of them!

Sunday — February 7

WE have a little rose arbour in our garden and our six-year-old visitor was very curious about it, despite the weather.

There's a willow circle pinned to the back of it with words painted on its backboard: *Peace, Love, Joy.*

He read the words carefully.

"Peace. Love. Joy. Where have I heard them? Oh, I know. Church!"

Any church would be pleased to have made a positive impression on a young mind in this time of multiple distractions.

But if we only find those fruits of the spirit within the walls of religious establishments then something has gone wrong.

Let's make a concerted effort not just to keep peace, love and joy for church, but also to take them out into the world, so that children might learn them wherever they are.

Monday — February 8

I DON'T know who our dear friend Mary had been talking to, but her demeanour suggested it hadn't been an uplifting encounter.

Then she gave herself a little shake and smiled.

"A bad attitude is like a flat tyre, Francis. You won't get anywhere until you change it."

Roses around the arbour – a pretty feature in any garden.

Tuesday — February 9

ROBIN generally keeps himself to himself. But he did tell the local window-cleaner he could refill his bucket there any time.

"Well, it ensures your own windows get cleaned with the freshest, soapiest water," I commented, having seen that hard-working gentleman just leave.

"You're right, it does," Robin agreed. "But I didn't think of that until afterwards."

And that, my dear friends, is how kindness works. In helping others, you almost always help yourself, whether you realise it or not.

Wednesday — February 10

THERE'S not much to laugh about these days, some say.
Ma Joad didn't have much to laugh about in John Steinbeck's "The Grapes Of Wrath". She had to sustain the family through the Great Depression on not much more than nothing.

Yet the author said of her, "It was her habit to build up laughter from inadequate materials."

Inadequate materials are what many of us have most of, so let's put them to good use and build some laughter.

Thursday — February 11

NORMAN lives on the Mull of Kintyre. He told me of the B842, the road that runs along the east side of that peninsula.

"Initially, I suspect, this would have been the royal route for the Lord of the Isles from Dunaverty Castle to his fortress in Skipness. Both those strongholds are now ruins and largely forgotten."

It reminded me of the poem "Ozymandias" where the inscription at the foot of a broken statue said, "Look on my works, ye Mighty, and despair!"

Looking around, all the reader saw was desert.

While the empire of Ozymandias and the castles of the Lords of the Isles rise and fall, ordinary people meet, get married, have children. Love and family go on regardless.

Friday — February 12

NIL ADMIRARI is a Latin phrase describing a person who was surprised by nothing. Some took it too far. Indeed, in an effort to be surprised by nothing, they determined to be impressed by nothing and rarely had a word of praise for anyone.

This attitude is, thankfully, no longer fashionable. Other than maintaining the individual's high impression of themselves, it benefited no-one.

How much better to be *admirari:* those who are amazed, who are impressed, and who raise others up by being so!

Saturday — February 13

I KNOW very little of C.L. Burnham except that he contributed the lyrics to a cantata called "The Coming Of The Flowers" in the late 1800s.

But these words, attributed to him, seem quite apt for our duller February days.

There is always sunshine, only we must do our part. We must move into it.

The sun still shines above the clouds.

If we can't see it, we might seek out those who shine for our benefit – or shine, ourselves, for the benefit of others.

Sunday — February 14

*M*ELODIOUS *birdsong floats in on the air*
Through my window, I hear such precision and flair,
Blackbirds' sweet trilling, joined by blue tit and thrush,
A fair feathered choir in the morning's hush.
The sweetest of songs all joined in one,
A gentle reminder that a new day's begun,
In perfect harmony with greenfinch and wren,
Their music first building, then dipping again,
From fence and from tree-tops they sing on and on,
Each playing their part in the world's greatest song.

Amanda-Jayne Lanceley

A roaring fire – the warming heart of every room.

Monday — February 15

THERE was a prisoner with two possessions – a pencil and a violin. With the pencil, he drew a face on the wall of his cell. Then another. And another. And another . . .

Once he had covered three walls of his cell, he took out his violin. Then, standing on the bed which was against the fourth wall, he played to his "audience".

Just because you don't have a ready-made audience for your music – whatever it might be – doesn't mean you can't create one.

Whether they are real or not, what matters is that you play!

Tuesday — February 16

IT can be difficult to find the good in our troubles. C.S. Lewis once explained the idea to a friend, using the example of a coal fire.

He imagined it in the kindling stage, thinking it was doing just fine, merrily burning up the paper and the sticks. All would have seemed well to that fire.

Then, from above, a weight of "rocks" falls on it. Things collapse, the flames almost go out. How like a catastrophe must that seem.

The newly kindled fire could never imagine the blaze it would become, fuelled by the coal that seemed such a burden at first.

When hard times descend, it's our excuse – and opportunity – to burn brighter!

Wednesday — February 17

LYNSEY is one of a group of cousins who meet at their aunt and uncle's house once a week

"It's great," she told me. "Delicious food, people I love and plenty of room to dance."

That caught my attention.

"And do you?" I asked.

"Of course," she replied.

A place to gather is an important part of hospitality. But, in providing a place to dance, where it is actually encouraged, Aunt and Uncle have surely raised hospitality to a fine art!

WHEN the facility was still in the planning stages, people living in the area were told it would be a temporary shelter for children aged nine to sixteen, with no other home to go to.

Of course, someone started a petition against it. But construction, finally, went ahead.

I pop over with gifts from time to time, but because security is a priority I meet with staff and never go beyond the front door.

After one such visit, walking into the early evening gloom, I saw a lighted window with the blinds left open. A flash of colour caught my eye. I realised this was a bedroom and there, on the foot of the bed, was a large Winnie-the-Pooh.

That brief glimpse into a difficult childhood made a big impact on my heart. Who could raise a petition against a child who needed the comfort of a teddy-bear in a strange place? No-one, I am sure.

There are many things we might feel we ought to take a stand against, some for good reason. But we should be careful.

It's easy to object to something based on a different lifestyle, different religion or different cultural practices. Before we do, we ought to at least make an effort to get to know the human being – and the teddies – involved in them.

HAVING taken our seats early, the Lady of the House and I watched the rest of the audience arrive for a musical performance in a local theatre.

She indicated a man and a woman, telling me they were married. I admitted I would never have thought it.

"They seem a mismatched pair."

"Mismatched or not," she assured me, "they have been married for twenty-something years."

I thought of the reasons my sweetheart, in younger years, might have considered me a poor match. Surely there weren't too many!

I comforted myself with the words of Shelley from his poem "Epipsychidion".

"Are we not formed as notes of music are, for each other though dissimilar . . .?"

Saturday — February 20

NATURE is perhaps not putting on her best display right now. The naturalist John Muir wrote, "When we try to pick out anything (in nature) by itself, we find it connected to the whole universe."

It's no less true in winter than it is in summer. And, dare I suggest, the same applies to us, both in season and out.

Sunday — February 21

TOWARDS the end of the 2006 children's film "Charlotte's Web" it is mentioned that, thereafter, the people of the town were happier, gentler, more patient, more loving. Why? Because they had seen miracles.

The "miracles" most of them thought they saw were words appearing in spider's webs, written there by Charlotte the spider.

Earlier, the farmer had said a spider's web was a miracle in its own right.

Looking to either side of me at the children engrossed in the movie, I knew that they were miracles as well.

I wondered at the difference it might make to us, and our place in the world, if only we understood we were seeing real, God-woven miracles all the time.

Monday — February 22

IT was a mixed weather sort of day, like we so often get at this time. There was sunshine and blue sky, but also dark clouds. There was warmth in the sun and a chill in the breeze.

Passing a field, I noticed the blimp-shaped shadow of a cloud lying diagonally across it.

There were about 30 cows in that field. Fifteen or so were in one sunlit corner and the others were in the other sunlit corner.

There were none in the middle.

What can we learn from this? Simply that, if someone or something throws shade on your happiness, then follow the example of that herd and moo-ve to brighter pastures!

BOTHWELLHAUGH was a mining village, situated in what is now Strathclyde Park.

None of the houses compared with neighbouring Hamilton Palace, one of the grandest homes in the land. But long after the palace was torn down and the colliery had closed, locals still referred to their village as "the Pailis."

A house doesn't have to be fancy to be a home.

And a home doesn't have to be architecturally significant to be a palace, or "pailis."

All it needs is to be loved by those who live there.

THEY erected a chalkboard and allowed locals and visitors to write on it at Fish Hoek Beach near Cape Town in South Africa.

I particularly liked these words from the chalkboard:

"The first to apologise is the bravest, the first to forgive is the strongest, and the first to forget is the happiest!"

I HAVE a motto on my wall
I see it every day,
It gives me hope for every task
And helps me on my way.

"Believe you can and you're halfway there,"
So simple, yet so true,
I tell myself so many times
That's all you have to do.

So when your problems crowd around
These are the words you need:
"Believe you can" – remember that
And know you will succeed!

Iris Hesselden

Tourists and locals in the sun.

Fish Hoek beach in Cape Town.

Friday — February 26

WHEN Laurence Sterne sought to dedicate "The Life And Opinions Of Tristram Shandy, Gentleman" to Lord William Pitt (the elder) he hoped the book would make him laugh.

Sterne was writing from an old cottage, struggling with ill-health and "other evils of the world".

Yet he was convinced that "every time a man smiles – but so much more when he laughs – it adds something to this fragment of life."

We all have our trials, but if, in the midst of them, we can cause another to smile, or laugh, then we will surely have won a victory against those woes and have made the world an ever-so-slightly better place.

Saturday — February 27

BENJAMIN JOWETT, Master of Balliol College in the late 19th century, wrote, "Many a one, being thought better than he was, has become better."

What does that take? It takes someone willing to give that individual a chance, willing to risk that they might be let down.

And, if we are let down, what shame is there in hoping for the best, in hoping to help create the best?

Better people in a better world . . . It's a risk worth taking, I think.

Sunday — February 28

JESUS addressed the issue in his parable of the Good Samaritan. Yet, there are still times when we are tempted to walk on by. We tell ourselves that, if we didn't help, at least we did no harm.

But there are other forces than good in the world, forces that need only the absence of good for their work.

The great Scottish novelist Robert Louis Stevenson, in a letter to his mother, wrote, "It is much more important to do right than not to do wrong: further, the one is possible, the other has always been, and will always be, impossible."

Given that neither Christ nor Stevenson believed in a neutral choice, choose, my friends, to do good!

March

HE was not born of a caring relationship. Legend has his abandoned mother giving birth to him on a rocky beach in a thunderstorm.

But, despite not being born of love, he still spread the message of God's love all across Wales, founding a monastery and becoming an archbishop in the process. How?

Well, St David had no technology to rely on (although a hill did, supposedly, raise him up so more people could see and hear him). But his message was one people could appreciate and pass on.

David, or Dewi Sant, as he is now known, taught simplicity in faith – a focus on doing the little things properly, as you would in the presence of God.

Can you imagine the difference it would make if we took that sort of care with the details of our own lives?

On St David's Day (and on every other day) we might all benefit from following the example of Wales's patron saint.

THE little lad was torn between joy over the gift and embarrassment at his mother urging him to say "Thank you".

He managed it, but the encounter left me wondering why we sometimes find those two words so difficult to say.

The 12th-century Persian poet Shams Tabrizi suggested we ought to give thanks even when it seemed that life was giving us nothing. Because that nothing would inevitably turn out to be a gift in its own right.

And I thought getting little boys to say thank you was difficult! Imagine if we not only had to say thank you for what we received, but also for what we didn't receive!

But it made me think. And for that, Shams Tabrizi, I thank you!

I CAN feel that it's coming –
There's a change in the air.
The barometer's showing
The weather set fair.
It may be too early
To hope that it's true,
Yet the dark skies of winter
Have begun to turn blue.
Life stirs in the garden
As spring now attends
With flowers returning
Like favourite old friends.

John Darley

I AM sure we can all appreciate the good things in life for their own sake.

Things like a nice home, a happy family and plentiful food are difficult to take for granted (although, sometimes we still manage to).

But to know the true value of a thing, try sharing it, even for a little while, with someone who doesn't have it.

It might cost you a little in the short term, but the rewards will be worth it in the long term.

Oliver Goldsmith was an Irish novelist, playwright and poet who lived and wrote in the 18th century.

His philosophical poem "The Traveller" is still considered a classic of mid-18th-century poetry.

In it, he described a fireside scene in a home that had provided temporary refuge for the traveller of the title.

Blest be those feasts with simple plenty crowned,
Where all the ruddy family around
Laugh at the jests or pranks that never fail,
Or sigh with pity at some mournful tale.
Or press the bashful stranger to his food,
And learn the luxury of doing good.

Friday — March 5

I **DO** like reading old books. I could see where the top of the spine had been worn away on this volume by frequent pulling from the shelf.

The black papers inside the cover made me think of old bibles.

A sticker there said it had been sold from a shop where there are no shops any more.

I opened it at random and put my nose to it. Ah, the owner had been a pipe smoker. Perhaps, also, a writer, because one page still bore a fingerprint in Indian ink.

From the date of publication, I guessed both the writer and original owner had long ago completed their stories.

These and other details I pored over, enjoying the experience thoroughly. Then, having read the book, I began on the words inside.

Saturday — March 6

I'**D** like to be nice to him," I muttered to the Lady of the House, "but he is just such a pain in the neck!"

"Perhaps he'd be less of a pain if you were nice to him."

"Aye, but why should I make allowances for his bad attitude? Surely he should change first. Oh, I don't know. Where does it begin?"

"It begins," my sweetheart gently assured me, "with the one willing to make the sacrifice."

Sunday — March 7

THALES of Miletus, who was one of the Seven Sages of ancient Greece, thought that "everything is full of gods", according to Aristotle.

Almost six centuries after Thales died, the Apostle John writing of Jesus said, "Through Him all things were made."

Some things are just known, deep in the soul, and people in different times find their own ways to put those truths into words. The essential message is the same.

Monday — March 8

WHILE browsing through an old book of Gaelic proverbs, I noticed a strange thing. The proverbs were spoken by poor folk, leading a precarious existence.

The book listed many ways the people might be wronged, but the spoken responses to those actions rarely involved hatred.

Instead, when they mentioned someone who might wrong a neighbour, a tenant or an animal, they began with "Pity him."

The implication was that the person concerned must be lacking in some way, or damaged. Why else would they do such things?

Pity and sympathy. Much healthier options than hate and retribution – with much greater scope for healing.

Tuesday — March 9

IN the early 1900s, the American poet Vachel Lindsay would trek across that vast country writing poems and exchanging them for food. Occasionally, he made money from them. Sometimes he made so much he had to send it home to keep his pockets light.

He had a list of self-imposed rules for these travels. Some were concerned with staying away from railroad and cities; some with the company he should or shouldn't keep.

But there were two rules anyone might benefit from taking on board.

"Be neat, deliberate, and civil" and "Preach the Gospel of Beauty."

Wednesday — March 10

THERE is a simple rhyming maxim from the Highlands of yesteryear that I am very fond of.

"The day is longer than the brae."

The "brae" is, of course, the hill.

People who often knew hardship must sometimes have thought their life was an uphill struggle.

But they also knew the value of perseverance and believed that if they only kept going they would get there.

Keep going. Climb higher than that brae!

AS we walked towards the hospital entrance, I stepped behind the Lady of the House so we could move, single file, through a busy area.

He came towards us, leaving the hospital, grimacing each time he took a step.

Still, he saw my sweetheart, stepped slightly to the side, and nodded as she passed by. I smiled and thanked him.

Two very small movements from a man I didn't know. So small I might not have noticed them.

But the step and the nod, even in his discomfort, were echoes of a "ladies first" attitude.

I mentioned my thoughts after our visits were complete.

"Old-fashioned courtesies and manners are still with us," the Lady of the House said. "It's just they are much more modest these days."

Friday — March 12

THERE, in my flower-bed,
In the corner I can see,
Bands of golden daffodils –
A sign of spring to me.

Nodding their pretty heads
In rhythm with the breeze,
Bringing colour to my garden
Beneath my apple trees.

Like a little army,
To attention they all stand,
Ready for my inspection –
They do look very grand.

A reminder of my Welsh roots
And that, like them, it's true,
As they grow afresh each year
I, too, can start anew.

Amanda-Jayne Lanceley

Saturday — March 13

TOM TIDDLER'S GROUND is an ancient children's game. One child plays the role of Tom Tiddler, with a defined patch of ground.

Then he must either catch, or chase away, the other children when they step into his domain.

Charles Dickens, in a short story, put a different spin on Tom Tiddler's Ground. The man referred to as Tom Tiddler scattered ha'pennies on his land for tramps who might be passing through.

To those gentlemen of the road the copper coins would have seemed like silver and gold. Thus, Tom Tiddler's ground became a richer place. And all through his charity.

Sunday — March 14

HOW many countries around the world celebrate Mother's Day, or Mothering Sunday? I did a quick count and came up with 140.

As someone said recently, "Women only make up half the population of the world today, but we gave birth to all of it!"

From the little things like comforting us when we cry, to the major things like ensuring the continuation of the species, we would all be lost without mothers and their wonderful works.

We have Mothering Sunday once a year. I suggest we look on that as a starting point. Celebrate your mother, or whoever stands in the place of a mother for you, as often as you can.

They deserve no less. In fact, they deserve much more.

Monday — March 15

COUNTLESS tales, cartoons and jokes depict a wise man sitting at the top of a mountain. "Seekers" will climb the mountain, ask a question, then be satisfied or confounded by the answer.

But perhaps we focus too much on the seekers' journeys and the wise man's answers.

The hill-top dweller has to be available to whomever would seek him. He is open to everyone, no matter their status, no matter how far they have travelled, no matter how wise or foolish their question.

And he graces each with the same consideration.

The world would be lost without mothers.

iStock.

SOME people wear you down. And that's not always a bad thing! Take Jim and Pete. Jim's financial situation hasn't been great for a while, but he gets by. And he has his pride.

When he was struggling a while back, his friend Pete, who lives too far away to help in person, sent him some money. Annoyed, Jim sent it back.

A holiday came and money arrived with a note saying to spend it on the children. He wasn't happy, but it was for the children . . .

A few days ago, he showed me books he'd bought with the money Pete sent him for his birthday.

He had a "Thank You" card to post.

"Not annoyed at him any more?" I asked.

"Ach," Jim replied. "He wore me down with kindness."

That's the best way to do it!

WHEN the storms of life are raging
And tumult's all around,
I hide beneath your feathers
To keep me safe and sound.

Your feathers come in many forms,
Soft and gentle as a dove;
Your spirit quietly speaks to me
And whispers songs of love.

It's there I find your comfort,
Your tender heart so strong;
You cover me completely
And hide me from the storm.

Then once again on eagle's wings
You teach my heart to soar,
To fly above the storms of life
And trust in you once more.

Marisa Rosie

Thursday — March 18

AN old Scottish tale has Alexander Stewart, the Earl of Mar, making his way home on foot after losing a battle. Exhausted and hungry, he begged a handful of barley-meal from a housewife.

Not wanting to endanger her by stopping at her house, he walked on until he reached a stream. He scooped up some water in his shoe, mixed the barley with the water and thereafter ate a meal so tasty he wrote a poem about it!

Can you imagine eating dinner from your shoe and then praising it in verse? Of course, it is need and appreciation that truly makes a meal, not what it is served in!

Friday — March 19

A MAN who had been driving all day pulled over to inspect a hand-made sign. *This is a long, slow, relaxing road.*

He saw a farmer nearby, nodded at the sign, and shouted: "It looks just the same as all the other roads I've been on. What makes this one different?"

"You do, I guess," the farmer said after a moment.

That imaginary road is like the journeys of our lives. In the main they are pretty similar.

What makes the difference is how we choose to travel them.

Saturday — March 20

WISDOM passed down through generations of farmers suggests that "One night in March is better than three days in August".

Why? Because even at night the world knows spring has begun.

It doesn't matter what the weather is like, or how nice those three days in August might be – when it's time to grow, growth will be achieved.

The tides, the waxing and waning of the moon, and growth in its proper season. A few of the things in this life we don't control.

So, on this first day of spring, we might as well relax and appreciate them!

Sunday — March 21

IN Robert Louis Stevenson's story "The Pavilion On The Links", Frank Cassilis travelled around Scotland with his worldly goods on a horse-drawn, two-wheeled cart. His "whole business" was always to seek out the desolate corners where he might live awhile.

Some of us might make it our business to spend as much time as possible in good company. Who's to say either of those options is a bad one? But perhaps the best option of all is to combine the two.

Enjoy the company of others, but always know of a nearby place where you can spend time with yourself.

Except you won't be alone. Creation will be with you – and God. But he is very congenial company and won't intrude unless invited.

Monday — March 22

WE have a romanticised view of crofters or farmers sitting down of an evening with the only illumination coming from the fire in the hearth. In certain parts of the country it would have been peat (or turf) burning, and there is a real feeling of cosiness about the image. One can almost smell it.

Why, then, is there an old expression, "The turf is a cold companion"?

Because, as hot as the fire might be, it is not actually a companion and there is no warmth like that of a friend who will sit with you. Nor many kindnesses as worthwhile as being that companion to someone else.

Worth remembering, even in these days of central heating.

Tuesday — March 23

YOU wouldn't live in one room of a house and leave the other rooms locked!

An old Indian tradition compares people to a four-roomed house. One room represents the emotional aspect of us, another the spiritual, then the mental, with the last being the physical.

It goes on to say that many people spend their lives in one "room". Balance, it suggests, comes from spending time in each of them. Even if only to keep them well aired!

A cosy fireplace
warms the soul.

iStock.

Wednesday — March 24

HIS day started with an argument. Deciding the day was already ruined, he messaged a friend to apologise for a mistake. He phoned the tax office. He crawled under the bath to fix a leak.

All things that might have spoiled a good day, but couldn't make this one any worse.

The friend didn't remember the mistake. The tax people sorted the problem in 10 minutes. The leak was fixed in 20.

When his wife came home he apologised for being a fool. She said she was used to it!

"Not such a fool," he told me, "that I can't see that even a good-for-nothing day can be good for a lot!"

Thursday — March 25

GOING green" is a popular phrase these days. We should all do more to protect the natural world – which will itself be going green now spring is here.

But which green? It might be fern green, forest green, lime green, moss green, pine green, emerald green . . . the list goes on and on.

Rather than just saying "green", how about learning and appreciating the differences?

And the best way to do that? Be out there, if you can, amongst all those beautiful, burgeoning shades. Go green!

Friday — March 26

A COOK once said, "It is bad meat which won't take salt".
Salt, which can sting if it gets into a wound, will also enhance the flavour of a cut of meat. Of course, some meals are beyond the power of condiments to save.

Likewise, we might suggest it is a poor sort of person who won't take criticism. Critical words (not maliciously spoken) can sting our pride when we first hear them. But they might also contain truth and wisdom we can benefit from and be enhanced by.

May we never be so "tough" we refuse to accept a little salt (or well-meant criticism) in our lives.

MY neighbour's garden is on a slope.
He wanted to place a hut there, but he wanted the floor of the hut, of course, to be level.

We laid a tarpaulin on the grass (away from the hut site), then we lifted turf and dug and raked.

The end result was a smooth, level, hut-sized area.

But the tarpaulin now had a hill of dirt on it.

I was concerned.

It wouldn't be easy to get rid of and, in the meantime, the grass under it would slowly be turning yellow. That was my attitude, anyway.

The mother of the family had a different view of what lay before us.

She produced a large, multi-coloured, hand-held windmill.

Then she organised their four-year-old son to come with her for an expedition up "the highest mountain in the world".

When the intrepid pair reached the top (after much exaggerated puffing and several over-dramatic tumbles) they planted the windmill – where it flew proudly until Daddy and I cleared the mountain away.

Life can be full of hard work and problems.

But there is surely, also, always a place for some heart-lifting nonsense.

Sunday — March 28

IMAGINE that you were a subsistence farmer a few centuries back, and you owned a field that might be farmed, but it was full of rocks.

Would your heart sink?

Not if you knew that the lichen growing on the rock was corcar or crotal, from which crimson and rust-coloured dyes might be made and an income earned.

All too often in this life, the difficulty isn't in the lack of opportunities, it's in not recognising the opportunities God places in front of us.

Playful fox cubs.

GREAT-AUNT LOUISA'S diaries refer often to countryside walks. In one she mentions watching the bracken shake and hearing the immature barks that told her fox cubs were at play there.

In another she records being close enough to a cuckoo to hear him wheezing just a little after an extended bout of cuckoo-ing. In a third she wrote of finding a mountain pansy in an area not known for them.

She ends these and other episodes with variations of the words, "We shared a moment of wonder, then we left them to it and made our way home."

Appreciation rather than interference. It makes sure the wonder is still there the next time you, or anyone else, ventures out into Mother Nature's realm.

IT was a cartoon that caught my eye, and my imagination. A little boy decided the summer sky was just too blue and could do with another colour. So he fetched his red kite and flew it!

I am usually one who encourages people to appreciate the natural world more, but that cartoon reminds me that we are not separate from nature; not just spectators. We are every bit as wonderful as the best day and, when days are less than beautiful, we are fully entitled to add something extra and, hopefully, worthwhile to them.

A PENNY wedding, in times gone by, was one where the newlyweds wouldn't have enough money to cover the cost of a wedding. Their friends were also likely to be poor, but if each of them contributed a penny, then the costs would be covered, with some left over to set up a home.

How much money came in would depend entirely on how popular the bride and groom were.

Never have I heard of a better, or more practical, description of how our true wealth is not in our wallets or bank accounts, but in our friends.

April

HAVE you ever listened to the song "April Showers" from the classic Disney animated film, "Bambi"?

It's a choral and orchestral piece, played as Bambi and his mother settle down to sleep in the forest. The whole night is displayed in five dramatic minutes: a few drops of rain fall, it gets gradually heavier, the rain turns into a storm, thunder rolls, lightning flashes . . . then morning breaks with rays of heavenly sunshine.

The voices of the choir are light and happy when singing "drip-drip-drop little April showers"; they are scary as they pretend to be howling winds; and they are full of awe as the clouds part and the sunshine returns.

All of those sounds are produced by the same voices.

How we use our voice and the effects we produce are up to us. Encourage people's interest (Bambi is fascinated by the raindrops), have them cower away, inspire awe and wonder.

You have the voice. It's all in how you choose to use it.

BOB ROSS, the host of the American TV show "The Joy Of Painting", enjoyed encouraging people to take up their brushes and paints. One day he had a letter from someone who said they could never be a painter because they were colour-blind.

Mr Ross was not content to leave it like that. So, on that day's programme, he created a beautiful mountain scene, with snow-capped peaks beneath a cloudy sky. A viewer might have admired the painting without thinking it in any way unusual – until they realised that it was painted entirely in shades of grey.

Whatever is stopping you from pursuing your dream might not actually be stopping you. It might just require that you look for different ways of achieving it.

Saturday — April 3

THE owner of a pest-control company recently went on to social media to announce he was giving his "employee of the month" a long weekend of fishing and relaxing at a cabin in the woods as a reward for his hard work.

It turns out the business is a one-man company. The owner is the employee, and vice versa!

I see a lot of comments saying that, to take care of others, you first have to take care of yourself. There is an element of truth to this, although some people use it as an excuse to focus on themselves.

As with all things, it's a matter of balance. If you've been working hard recently, and if you would do it for an employee, then why not reward yourself?

Be your own employee of the lifetime, with commensurate, appreciative rewards!

Sunday — April 4

A BOY I know is scared to walk past a particular garden in case the dog barks.

Gathering his courage, he told me, "I won't be afraid of it when I am bigger. But that dog's as big as it's going to get."

Though tender in years and innocence, he had stumbled on a great truth. Our fears are what they are. It's up to us to outgrow them.

Monday — April 5

THE longer days, the sun's warm rays,
No gardener can ignore,
And as light spreads, the flower-beds
Grow colourful once more.
It satisfies to cast one's eyes
On such a pleasant scene,
Where spade and hoe and what you sow
Can turn your fingers green!

John Darley

Tuesday — April 6

HE sought me out after hearing me give a talk.

"I give money to the charity you were telling us about. It's no big deal – I have plenty and there's no denying it's a good cause. I'd get more involved but I'm too busy.

"What I wish, though . . . I wish I got the buzz out of it that you so obviously do."

I was diplomatic. I thanked him for the financial support and told him it helped a lot of people.

What I didn't say was that, if he wanted to give in a way that meant more to him, perhaps he ought to give something that actually cost him.

Not the money he had so much of, but perhaps the time of which he seemed to have so little.

Wednesday — April 7

THE Maori language is an ancient one, but in 2017 a new word was added as part of a mental health programme. *Takiwatanga* means autism in Maori. It also means, "in his or her own space and time."

It's a beautiful and hopefully helpful concept for a situation so many people are living with; one that, if we all adopted it, would ease many lives.

What's to stop us extending the courtesy? After all, our own space and time is all any of us have.

Thursday — April 8

AGED eighty-three, Peter started going along to a day-care centre near his home. He was lonely since his wife died and was looking to make new friends. And he did.

It was only after he left the first time that he realised the centre was built on the site of his old primary school – where he had once gone into the playground in search of new friends.

The realisation made him laugh out loud.

"Friends," he said. "It seems we never outgrow our need for them."

Friday — April 9

ST FRANCIS of Assisi once said that when we leave this life, we take nothing with us that we have received – only that which we have given.

Likewise, in this life, possessions, while good in moderation, will eventually weigh us down. Our worries for them might eventually outstrip the pleasure in them.

But the things we give, the good we do? They weigh nothing at all, and they are out there helping others who might in turn lighten our load.

Give and you shall receive. Plus, you'll have less to carry!

Saturday — April 10

I'VE a young friend who thinks the best game in the world is to sneak up behind me and shout, "Boo!"

Whether I see her coming or not, I always jump and act flustered. And she laughs and laughs.

This little game has been played out maybe 100 times, and people ask me if it doesn't get annoying.

I settle for saying "No", but what I want to say is, "No, because I am not yet so old that I have forgotten how wonderful a thing childhood delight is." And I hope I never do.

Sunday — April 11

FOUR-YEAR-OLD Aiden and six-year-old Rory were having fun with a cardboard box. They sat the box on the bed, climbed inside it, and then tipped it until it fell off the bed.

The crash as it hit the floor alerted their mum, Shona. She rushed upstairs to find the boys climbing back into the box on the bed and immediately told them to stop.

"You could hurt yourself," she told them.

"It's OK," Aiden assured her. "Rory holds my head and I hold his."

Shona's not sure that plan will greatly decrease their chances of getting hurt. But she does hope the boys continue to grow up with each other's wellbeing firmly in their hands.

Monday — April 12

THE puddle filled the path. The grass on either side had been turned to mud by people taking the long way around it.

I remembered the words of an older friend.

"A lot of folk will slip and fall, skirting the edges, trying not to get wet. But if you have sturdy shoes with a good sole, you might as well walk through.

"You won't slip, and you'll come out with clean shoes."

It seemed like a mini-sermon to me.

Make sure all is well with your soul, and keep walking the straight path home!

Tuesday — April 13

YOU might not have heard of the Lochy unless you live in the area. It is a Scottish river that enters the sea near the base of Ben Nevis.

It is not particularly noteworthy, but the people who knew it, in days gone by, said, "The sea is bigger because of the Lochy".

The good you do might seem insignificant. Most people won't hear of it.

But, as the Lochy increases the sea, so your kindness will make the world a better place.

Wednesday — April 14

WRITER and comedian Barry Cryer was on BBC Radio 4 talking about kindness. On a previous guest slot he had discussed the importance of silliness.

Trying to find a word that combined the two things, he found himself at a loss.

So the presenter of the show asked if the listeners could come up with one.

There were several responses, but the first was my favourite: Humanity.

Silly and kind. I don't know about the rest of humanity, but I would settle for that!

ONCE upon a time the metals were torn from the earth, plastics were processed from oil and rubber was taken from trees or produced artificially.

Mighty industrial processes formed them into a car which, for some reason, someone drove into a wooded area and abandoned.

It has been there perhaps 30 years and there is not much left of it.

The sun has made the plastics brittle and prone to turn to dust, and the metals are being washed by the rain back into the soil.

A tree now grows between where the two front seats were.

I sit on a nearby stump from time to time and study it, reassured that time heals and that Mother Nature is the best recycler ever.

Of course, we needn't make it any more difficult for her!

SHE looked about seven years old, with long red hair. She was wearing a Wonder Woman costume.

She shuffled her feet, played with her hair and watched the other children playing in a group.

They were about a dozen feet away from her and couldn't have missed her, but for whatever reason, she wasn't included in their games.

I wanted to talk to her.

"I know it feels awful. But it doesn't matter.

"You are already ahead of the game. You are a watcher, which almost always means you are a thinker. You don't automatically submerge yourself in the group mentality.

"Already, in trying to understand why they belong and you don't, you are a student of human nature. Those others will probably always do what everyone else does. But you will do you.

"Not instinctively fitting in to whatever group happens to be around, you will be an individual. You will be the best you can be, not limited by other people's expectations.

"When you are seven, this hurts, but you are already a wonder, if only you could see it."

A good group of friends can be as close as family.

Saturday — April 17

THE gang meet in a café every Friday. They have coffee, tea, toasties and cakes, and they put the world to rights.

This day they were bemoaning the loss of "proper" mealtimes, where families sat at a table together, shared a meal and talked.

"Actually, when you think about it, we're sitting at this table and eating," Dave said. "Well, we're like a family, aren't we?"

Silence. Then someone nodded. Someone else said, "You're right."

We can bemoan the loss of things, or we can recreate them for the world we live in now.

Sunday — April 18

A BOY and a girl, both with long hair, were walking to school on a windy day. The boy kept turning his face away from the wind, with the result that he got a faceful of flapping hair.

It didn't add to his day, or his view!

The girl, however, kept her face turned towards the wind and her hair was swept out behind her.

Life. It's like having long hair on a windy day. How you face it makes all the difference!

Monday — April 19

THE waitress brought us two bowls of soup. Her boss watched her all the way from the kitchen to the table.

After she left, I whispered to my companion.

"I'd hate to work somewhere the boss scrutinised your every move like that."

When we paid, the boss asked how our soup was and how his daughter had done, adding he'd been concerned she might burn herself with the soup.

Ah! He wasn't scrutinising; he was being a concerned father.

Likewise, Biblical commandments can seem pretty strict. But it depends on how you see the writer.

A demanding boss, or a concerned Father?

As the sky spreads out its treasure
And the earth gives up her gift,
In unexpected timeless measure
I feel my spirit lift.
A winter, hard as we have known,
At last makes way for spring,
The earth, once hard as granite stone,
Now green and flourishing.
I feel the air warm on my skin,
I turn my face towards the sky;
All around new life begins.
I spread my wings and start to fly.

Elizabeth Brown

I OVERHEARD a woman questioning our friend Mary's take on life.

"Why must you always make more of things than they really are?"

Mary looked at the rings on the other woman's fingers.

"Are those real diamonds? Real gold?" They were.

Mary asked if she cleaned them. The woman said yes.

"Why do you do that?" she was asked.

"Well, because, in the natural course of things, they might get a bit grimy, a bit dull. Which is a shame, because underneath that they are really quite beautiful."

DO you like getting a good return for your money? You'll love what good deeds do.

If you lift someone's spirits with a kindness, you not only make their day, but you improve the day of everyone they come into contact with after that.

A return rate higher than any financial investment, and it might not even cost you a penny!

HIS face was gaunt, he walked with a stoop and he carried an old suitcase. He was too late for a foodbank parcel, but they managed to get some fresh veg and a few tins together for him. He put them into his suitcase through a hole burst in the side of it.

I shook his hand and wished him all the best.

He looked me up and down.

"I hope things get better for you, too."

I was confused. Then I realised. I was wearing old paint- and plaster-spattered clothes – ones I keep for doing messy work in. I had been doing some tiling in the church.

Of course, he didn't know what I'd been doing, or that I had other clothes at home. Likewise, I had no idea what had brought him to this point in his life. Judge not!

"Thank you, my friend. I really appreciate that!"

And my day did get better.

Saturday — April 24

I HAD two minutes to fill, so I picked a hardback book from the shelf. I looked at the plain blue fabric of the cover.

I had always thought the front of this particular book was undistinguished, with the information on the spine instead.

When I turned it, the lamplight picked out shadows.

When this book, "The Vailima Papers", had been new, a facsimile of Robert Louis Stevenson's signature had been pressed into the front of it.

Judging by the wording on the spine, it would have been "written" in gold.

Time and use had worn the name and the flourish underneath it away. But the impression remained.

When we do something for someone, it generally produces its golden moment: that time of thanks, of appreciation and feeling good.

Of course, that fades, as it should, and we move on.

But if what you did was good, done in the spirit of love, the impression will remain, even if few other than God ever see it.

Sunday — April 25

I **SHOOK** my head in despair at the mess.
A man was out with a dustpan and brush, sweeping up the broken bits of his car's rear light.

There had been no other cars in the area, and there was no other damage. It looked like someone had deliberately smashed the light.

"Some people seem to need to make the world worse," he said.

Two hours later, I walked through the same car park. The broken Perspex was all gone, along with the litter and everything else that shouldn't have been there. The car park had been swept clean.

He forgot to say what he already knew. Which was that some people – most people – just seem to need to make the world better.

Monday — April 26

A **FRIEND** of Harry's gave him a notebook she made at a book-binding workshop. He showed me. It was beautifully made; covers like honey, the spine a dark green and the pages neatly stitched.

"A gift for you to record your thoughts in," she told him. But it has sat on his shelf since then.

"Every time I begin to write," he told me, "I worry that my words won't be good enough. Yet I feel free to speak to people every day.

"I don't mean we should let fear of saying the wrong thing keep us silent. Quite the contrary. But maybe we could think more about what we say. If the words aren't constructive enough to be included in a hand-crafted notebook, why unleash them on a beautiful world?"

Tuesday — April 27

G **EORGE** is proud to say his daughters volunteer with charities.
"I like to think I raised them to feel that giving back to society is important," he said. "Of course, they each think they came up with the idea themselves! Ah, well. The flower never remembers the hand that planted the seed. "

And that's the way it should be.

WAS tempted to think him a fool. He was teaching people how to play "The Blue Danube" on piano, but he couldn't pronounce it.

"Is it Danooby? Is it Dan-yoobay?"

He was American. Why would he know a European river?

A German friend told me they called it the Donau. It runs through 10 countries so probably has several names. It was a reminder that, when we judge people, we leave ourselves open to be judged.

And he played it beautifully, whatever it was called.

DIDN'T even realise I did that," Bob said, slightly embarrassed. I know Bob from church and had spoken to him after the service.

"If the pastor says something special, or a member of the congregation speaks up, or if there's a moment's silence where no-one quite knows how to respond, you will start the round of applause.

"And everyone else will join in."

How many will risk the possibility of no-one else joining in just to make sure someone feels appreciated?

Barnabas, a follower of Jesus, was known as "the son of encouragement". The world needs more encouragers.

Barnabas, Bob and . . . can I add your name to that list?

H.L. GEE'S book, "This Kind World" lay in a box of books at a car-boot sale. I picked it up and read the inscription.

Happy birthday to one of the kindest people in this kind world. Olive.

I wish I had known what they had done for Olive to think so highly of them. I looked at the date beneath the inscription. *10/03/49.*

Olive might have left this world by now, for all I know. But the ink looked like it had been freshly laid on the paper.

That's the thing about acts of kindness. They are for ever fresh!

May

A DAUGHTER is so special,
She sits within your heart,
From the moment she's laid in your arms
Until it's time to part.
And even as she says goodbye
And, smiling, walks away,
A daughter's love will travel
With you each and every day.

Linda Brown

DID you rise up early yesterday to wash your face in the Mayday dew? Have you been duly beautified? Never having partaken of the ritual, I couldn't vouch for the restorative properties of the dew on that particular day, but there is something uplifting about the idea of starting the day, even if only once a year, in such a fashion.

The early morning has a quality of its own, something worth experiencing more often. It is a time of potential, a time of connection.

A time of purpose, to set your course for the day ahead.

In rising early, we have already achieved something, which must bode well for the day ahead.

The Swedes, so I hear, have a word that describes the practice of getting up early specifically to hear the birds sing. It's called *gökotta* and you can do it any time of the year, although the birds do tend to be more vocal in the summer months.

Of course, you might be tempted to succumb to the charms of a longer lie abed . . .

Deliberately starting your day off with something of nature, something of beauty, that has to be better than the last-minute clamour of the alarm clock, don't you think?

SHE would be well past retirement age – if she could afford to retire.

She sells household items, door to door, from a big carry-all. I've bought a few things from her and we have gradually exchanged more and more words as we've got to know each other better.

This particular day was a miserable one.

I asked her how she was, expecting the usual "fine".

But, instead, she smiled.

"Oh, I don't like to cry in the face of the Lord. I'm walking and I'm talking, so I'm blessed."

And off she went on her rounds, praying, as I knew from previous conversations, for everyone who shut the door on her.

The walk of faith at its most practical!

Tuesday — May 4

YOU could walk through Pando in south-central Utah thinking it was a forest of Quaking Aspen trees.

Actually, it isn't a forest but one tree, joined by an immense root system. Pando is thought to be one of the largest and oldest organisms in the world.

It only looks like a whole bunch of separate trees – just as we look like separate people when, actually, we are all related and all part of the one "organism" known as humanity.

Wednesday — May 5

THE Garden of Cosmic Speculation in Dumfriesshire is a private garden and also a spectacular work of art.

It is open to the general public one day a year and raises money for charity.

If you aren't lucky enough to get a ticket, why not sit in your own garden, or on a patch of wild land, and take the time to properly savour it.

The closer you look at what grows there and what lives there, the more "cosmic" it will seem.

Time communing with nature is always time well spent.

Thursday — May 6

JAMIE is a drystane-dyker. I stood with him as he considered a sizeable gap in an old stone wall he'd been hired to repair. The original materials had long since disappeared.

"You'll be needing some big rocks for this job," I offered.

"I could do without the backache," he said with a dismissive laugh. "Besides, my grandad taught me that the biggest holes in a dyke can be filled with little stones – if you have the patience."

A philosophy, I thought, that was good for more than fixing walls. Many a large problem can be resolved a little bit at a time, if you have the patience to keep going until it's done.

Friday — May 7

YOU are wonderful, you know," I said to Harry.

"Oh, come on." He dismissed my praise with a wave. "It was a little thing I did. That's hardly worth such flowery praise."

"You did a little thing today," I said, not letting him off the hook. "You did another little thing yesterday. There was that little thing you did the day before . . ."

"You make such a fuss," he said.

Taking pity on his embarrassment, I let the subject drop.

But, you know, my favourite people aren't necessarily the ones who do some great thing; they are more usually the ones who do the little things – and keep on doing them!

Saturday — May 8

I DON'T know what kind of hedge it was but I stopped and stared a while anyway.

The branches seemed never to have grown far in a straight line, twisting and entangling repeatedly.

In some places they seemed to have actually tied themselves in knots.

But you know what? Despite all of that, the blossom coming forth from those branches was beautiful.

Don't be constrained by your circumstances. Be beautiful anyway.

HE waved and said, "Hi, how you doing? Haven't seen you for a long time."

I certainly had never seen him before.

"I'm fine? How are you?" I merely replied.

He told me some inconsequential stuff. Then, in response to some gentle questioning, he told me a heart-breaking story. We discussed it for a while, then he left, a lot less stressed.

If I had said "We've never met", no doubt he would have apologised and walked on – but he wouldn't have been able to unburden himself like he did.

Reaching out to one another, especially in difficult times, is a deep part of our human nature. Even if we can't help practically when someone does that, we can still help emotionally, by allowing the other person to share what might be too much for one person to carry – whether we know each other or not.

Monday — May 10

MY garden is my happy place,"
A friend once said to me,
"If ever I feel sad or down
It's where I love to be.

I feel as if it reaches out,
Enfolds me in embrace.
It steals away my gloomy thoughts,
And fills my heart with grace."

May all of us find spaces, too,
Good places of our own,
Where weeds of woe just shrivel up,
And seeds of hope get sown.

This world has many corners still
To offer us a base,
In which to find a sanctuary,
Our special Happy Place.

Maggie Ingall

Tuesday — May 11

AT a beauty spot in Tennessee, a tourist board has installed binocular-style viewers for people to enjoy the scenery through. But one is different from the others. It has built-in filters to allow people who are colour-blind to see the landscape the way others do.

Can you imagine how wonderful it must be, seeing nature as it was meant to be for the first time? The question that comes to mind after that has to be, why would those of us who can see it like that any time we like ever lose that sense of wonder?

Wednesday — May 12

HE had been given half a loaf of bread.
"If I had some electricity, I could make toast," he said.

"I have electricity but don't have bread," the man next to him said. "If you want to come to mine . . ." There was a moment of consideration and mutual agreement.

Then the woman sitting in the next seat turned.

"I have butter."

Someone once told me that the letters of "team" were an acronym for "together each achieves more".

These three, who individually had very little, as a team achieved hot buttered toast!

Thursday — May 13

IF you lay ten matches side by side and you ignite one of them, they will all burn. If you have six little steel balls hanging in a Newton's Cradle and you swing the first, the impact travels through the next four and sends the sixth swinging.

But if you remove a match, if you remove a ball, the damage or the impact stops there.

Matches and "steelies" don't have a choice in whether they stay or they go, but we do.

If you hear malicious gossip or fear-mongering coming your way, step aside, remove yourself, don't pass it on.

And you will stop the negativity right there!

There are few things nicer than hot buttered toast!

Friday — May 14

LOVE! I hope and pray that we all know what it feels like, but what do you think it looks like?

The great theologian St Augustine had this to say on the matter.

"It has the hands to help others. It has the feet to hasten to the poor and needy. It has the eyes to see misery and want. It has the ears to hear the sighs and sorrows of men. That is what love looks like." So, a bit like you and me – I hope!

Saturday — May 15

HOW would you react if a doctor prescribed regular doses of *Solvitur Ambulando*? It sounds like it could be the name of an impressive medication.

You needn't worry. It is actually a Latin phrase which is often taken to mean "The best way to figure out how something works is to try it out". But, there's more to it. In English, it means "it is solved (or cured) by walking".

Often, when our body is engaged in the process of walking, our mind is free to wander and wonder. Answers to problems that previously appeared insurmountable often occur to us when our minds have that freedom.

Then, of course, there are the many health benefits of a good walk.

Doctors would, I am sure, prescribe *Solvitur Ambulando*, or a good walk, as the cure for a good many things. And we would be wise to take it if we can.

Sunday — May 16

MAY I ask how you are feeling? Are you a bit gibbous? Bulbous? Waxing? Waning? Fading away? Full? Half-and-half?

Of course, you will have spotted that my descriptions are all phases of the moon.

But, as a wise person whose name escapes me once said, "The moon is a constant reminder that, no matter which phase we are in, we are always whole."

THE little girl ran up to the minister after Sunday school, just as he was about to send us out with a prayer.

"I made this for you," she said, handing him something.

"Well, thank you," he replied. "I'll treasure it."

"Oh, no, don't do that!" she shouted as she ran past him to join her parents. "Enjoy it!"

I wonder what she thought the expression "treasure it" meant. Perhaps she had seen cartoon pirates burying their treasure – or fighting over it.

Too many of the things we regard as treasure end up "buried" in a safe place, like a bank vault. Of use in monetary terms, but no use at all in terms of our soul, our charity, our joy of life.

Treasure, instead, the moments when a child gives you something in love; the opportunities to pass love and kindness on to another; time spent with family; the moments you can make someone feel welcome. Live your treasures, don't bury them.

IN 1910 Rudyard Kipling published a collection that included the poem "The Way Through The Woods". In it, the poet told of a path, once well used, that had been neglected.

First it became impassable, then it disappeared. There was no longer a way through the wood.

I was reminded of the Kipling poem when I saw a sign that read *1968 Girl Scout Tree Planting*.

The saplings the girls planted in the Sixties had grown to maturity. Now, not only was there a wood, but there was also a neatly maintained path through it.

A stroll between the trees and under a leafy canopy is one of my favourite things. I am convinced it does us all sorts of good. Not everyone gets the opportunity, unfortunately, but in my opinion everyone should.

If we would miss walks in the woods, perhaps we should follow the Girl Scouts' example and make sure there are woods.

Then find, and maintain, the ways through them.

Wednesday — May 19

IN the first half of the 20th century, the poet Sarah Teasdale wrote about a philosopher. He was a man in his nineties who seemed to have nothing of material value and yet, when she looked at him, it seemed that his eyes still danced with unquenchable youth.

She asked him his secret and he told her it consisted of only two things.

"I make the most of all that comes, and the least of all that goes."

A philosophy from which we all might benefit.

Thursday — May 20

KEN is an early riser.
"Some people rely on coffee, but I like to drink a cup of sunshine in the morning to brighten myself up," he told me.

I pointed out that our climate didn't always guarantee such shiny cuppas. He said he still sought it out, even on cloudy days.

"Some people have milky coffee, some have it dark; the effect is the same."

Perhaps, I thought, it's the searching after the sunlight that keeps Ken bright, rather than the sunlight itself.

Friday — May 21

IN the north-east of Scotland, in days gone by, an agricultural worker might sit on the chest of corn from which the horses were fed and sing of his day's work, or his relationship with the farmer, or any number of things.

He might beat his feet on the chest to keep time.

Some of these "cornkisters" became favourites, and the worker might perform his own song at a variety of farms, adding or dropping verses depending on who listening and who was in or out of favour.

These days, people prefer diaries or online posts, but imagine if you could record your days in song.

And imagine you lived such a life that you never had to drop a verse, no matter who was listening!

We are all seeking the sunlight in our journey through life.

*A*NEW life to love, a new care to give,
A new little person, who's got life to live,
A whole new beginning for him and for you,
So much to teach him and so much to do.

A perfect new grandchild, a whole brand-new start,
He's there, and already he's wrapped round your heart.
So now you are grandpa or grandma or gran,
A world to enjoy with this tiny young man.

Linda Brown

*A*LAN puts the minimum of effort into his allotment. He doesn't like the location, he says – it is at the bottom of a slope.

When it rains the ground floods, though others say it gets soggy!

He believes it is poor ground and that more than the minimum would be wasted effort.

Bryan's allotment is uphill from Alan's. He works hard at keeping it beautiful and productive. But he wishes he had Alan's patch.

Why? Because half of the compost and expensive enriching materials he uses gets washed downhill with the rain.

Alan's soil gets the benefit of it for free. It turns out Alan's land isn't "poor". Perhaps it simply suits him to think it is.

How often do we shape the world, the news, other people, towards our own inclinations? Sometimes it's our outlook that could do with enriching.

*T*HERE was a hand-written note on the church noticeboard.

One of the things I love most about this church is the little acts of kindness that are constantly happening.

Don't know what I mean? Look around! Or add some yourself. You'll be in good company. To which another writer had added, *Yes, you'll be in God's company.*

Tuesday — May 25

OLGA was at the Usher Hall in Edinburgh enjoying a wonderful performance by the Canadian classical pianist Angela Hewitt.

The audience gave a standing ovation, then Ms Hewitt returned the favour, giving them a round of applause.

Anyone who steps on a stage will tell you the audience is an essential part of the performance, and deserves appreciation.

In everyday life there are people who will do the equivalent of stepping on the stage. They reach out to help others; leave their comfort zone to make a difference; try to make the world better.

If no-one responds to what they do, they might lose heart, but a positive response might just be what keeps them going.

If you aren't inclined towards the performing life, at least you can fill the hall with your applause. The "performers" will appreciate it.

Wednesday — May 26

WE sang a song of May times when I was just a child,
When sunny days meant freedom from the classroom to the wild,
Where daisy chains were strung into bright circles for our hair
And we had our playtime snack outside and breathed God's good fresh air.

Ankle socks and dresses replaced the winter wool,
From finding ants to bumblebees, our days were very full,
'Midst buttercups and blossom, though our patch of grass was small,
We were in our heaven, there, behind the old school wall.

No matter that the playground flags were cracked beyond belief,
In our tiny garden, the tree was in full leaf,
We'd sit beneath its canopy, delighted from the start,
For Miss would read us poems – they shot straight into my heart.

The memories come flooding back, and every time, I smile
And I thank God for those May times when I was just a child.

Marian Cleworth

ROBERT STEPHENSON is generally remembered as the inventor of Stephenson's Rocket. His father, George, was also a successful engineer, something, surprisingly, he added to his son's list of credits.

In a biography by Samuel Smiles, George said, "When Robert was a little boy, I saw how deficient I was in education. I made up my mind, so that he should not labour under the same defect, that I should send him to a good school."

George was referring to formal education, of course. But there really is nothing like a child, and its fresh take on . . . everything, for reminding the rest of us of how little we know about the world. And for encouraging us to learn more.

Friday — May 28

A WISE man, whom you might not have heard of but who occasionally has coffee with me, had this to say.

"It's like the words that come out my mouth fall in front of me and pave the path I walk along. I need to ask myself, do I want to walk on thorns, or on rose petals?"

Saturday — May 29

THE Scots folk song "Birnie Bouzle" was written by James Hogg, the Ettrick Shepherd, in or around 1810. Within its lines, a young man asks a girl to marry him and lists the reasons why she would never regret it.

I had never heard it before. But Hogg wrote it, and various people sang it at ceilidhs or at the hearths of friends and family.

Aggie Stewart heard it on one such occasion and performed it in the 1950s. Isabel Sutherland heard it from her and recorded it.

Norman Buchan heard Ms Sutherland sing it and he included the lyrics in his book "101 Scottish Songs".

Reading that volume, published in 1962, brought the two-centuries-old song to my attention. And I thoroughly enjoyed it.

Put a pen to paper, or raise a voice in song. You might just be giving a gift to the ages.

Sunday — May 30

PETE and Susan's daughter, Nicole, had been in a car crash three weeks before. She'd been shaken and bruised but she had recovered well. After hospital appointments and visits from concerned parents, life went on as normal.

Pete had finally got around to repairing his own car's broken radiator grill. Because the grill was delivered by post it arrived wrapped in a substantial amount of protective packaging.

"At least you'll have plenty of bubble-wrap for wrapping up your precious things," he joked, tidying up afterwards.

"Like Nicole," Susan said without missing a beat.

"It was a throw-away comment," Pete told me afterwards. "We'd been talking about plenty of other things that morning. Nicole wasn't uppermost in the list of things I was thinking about that day.

"But, she was the very first thought Susan had when I mentioned precious things. Mother love, eh?"

Where would we be without it?

Monday — May 31

SOME people are particular about how they put their cups away. Others don't care if those cups sit bottom-up or bottom-down.

I never dreamed there'd be a deep significance to that simple act.

Apparently, in Nepal, after the last drink of the day the cup is put away bottom-up, or closed, to signify the ending and completion of the day. After a day well lived, there should be some satisfaction in this simple act.

In the morning, the cup is turned up, or open, signifying that it and its owner are ready to receive what the day has to offer. This would be accompanied by a sense of trust and anticipation.

Christians might easily take the tradition to their hearts, up-ending their cup with these words from Matthew.

"Therefore do not worry about tomorrow, for tomorrow will worry about itself."

And lifting it upright again the following morning to the words of the Psalmist.

"This is the day the Lord made. We will rejoice and be glad in it."

June

JAMES RUSSELL LOWELL, one of the American Fireside Poets, was obviously a fan of this month. He once asked, "And what is so rare (or special) as a day in June? Then, if ever, come perfect days!"

High praise! Of course, what constitutes a perfect day might be different for each of us. For some, tranquillity is the necessary ingredient, for others it might be the laughter of children.

For some it might be solitude, for others nothing will suffice but the company of a loved one. One might require an island beach, while another will be content with a good book and shade to read it in.

The perfect day, in detail, is very hard to define. But, in general, I'm with Mr Lowell.

June does give us some very fine days indeed. Then it's up to us to fill in the details that make them perfect!

THERE'S a halo that's waiting in heaven
For the many good deeds that you do,
For the kind things you say, in your own special way
And the times you don't focus on you.
When you've bypassed your own needs for others,
To help them and make sure they're fine;
Given up your seat, helped a man in the street,
Let your neighbour go first in a line.
So find comfort in opting for kindness,
Coming second will cause you no pain.
Count your blessings each day, for all God's brought your way,
As it's by giving back, we all gain.
When you've friends by your side, this life's journey is bright.
Sharing's caring, they say – and they're totally right!

Judy Jarvie

Thursday   June 3

MAKING a difference for the better can be difficult for some who think they might not have the resources. But, most often, the resources are far less important than the will.

The great Scottish writer J.M. Barrie highlighted this when, as an old man, he complimented a young friend in a letter.

Your first instinct is always to tell Jones the nice thing Brown said about him to Robinson; you have sown a lot of happiness that way.

Friday — June 4

I HAVE a Book of Days published in 2004, and a New Book of Days published in 1941. Hmm.

Books of Days began as a way of recording religious festivals and Saints' Days. These days, they are often collections of folk wisdom. True to their names, they will have at least one entry for every day of the year.

Now, what would happen if the compilers found that, from time to time, nothing much happened on those days? Would they leave blank pages? Or look a little harder?

Our lives are living books of days. We should try our best to make sure none of the "pages" are empty. If it seems like one might be, look a little harder!

Saturday — June 5

A TALE is told of the sons of William the Conqueror. As a character test, they were asked which bird they saw themselves as.

"A hawk," Robert Courthose replied, "because it is gallant and courteous like a knight."

"An eagle, because it is the king of birds and feared by them all," William Rufus replied.

The third surviving son, Henry Beauclerc, chose a starling.

"Because it lives simply, without robbing or hurting its neighbours."

In a simplistic summary of history, hawk and eagle often fought, but the sparrow succeeded them both. Worth thinking about?

These blossoms urge us to stay awhile.

iStock.

Pollok House in Glasgow.

Sunday — June 6

GREATER love hath no man than this; that a man lay down his life for his friends." Jesus said it, and who am I to argue.

On the same theme, today I saw a woman who'd been going about her business sit down on the pavement, just so a hurt and crying woman, whom she did not know, could rest against her breast and be wrapped in her arms until help arrived.

That's pretty good, too, if you ask me!

Monday — June 7

I AM glad I don't live in a stately home! But there is one in our area I like to visit. The gardens are beautiful and well maintained. I walk them for a little exercise, but my favourite thing is to find a bench, sit there, and read a book.

Really, though, any garden would do for that.

And it reminds me of the Chinese proverb, "A book is like a garden in your pocket."

Tuesday — June 8

DO you like to be right? Then, let me ask you, what sort of right do you like to be?

Do you prefer the kind where the people you surround yourself with and the publications you read all agree with you, and you with them?

The sort of right that is so sure of itself that it never needs to change?

Or the kind where you have stepped away from your own certainty for long enough to consider the other view, and what it might mean to the people who hold it?

The sort that is prepared to grow and change with new information and new understanding?

One of these is easy and satisfying, the other is more difficult and often troubling.

Both can be seen as right. The question is, what sort of right do you want to be?

ARE you one of those hardy souls who collects food from the seashore? If so, you will know we are coming into whelk season.

"Tis a bare beach when the whelks can be counted," an old proverb says.

Now, whelks are small and a lot might be found in a small area, so an "uncountable" number of them might soon be reached on many beaches.

Still, the humble whelk will be affected by pollution like most marine life and I sincerely hope they are still found on all of our island's beaches.

If nothing else, the proverb is a humble reminder that, left to its own devices (or even with some gentle stewardship), nature provides more than enough.

Thursday — June 10

MUCH has been written about the lives and attributes of great leaders. And, surely, they are different from the rest of us.

But this thought, from John Quincy Adams, the sixth President of the United States, suggests that each of us "ordinary people" might fulfil a similar role.

"If your actions inspire others to dream more, learn more, do more, and become more," he wrote, "then you are a leader."

Friday — June 11

THE power of love is an often-used theme for poets.

"You need power to do a wrong thing," the comic genius Charlie Chaplin is said to have written. "For everything else, love will suffice."

Can you imagine how different the world would be, if all its leaders and influencers affirmed love as the only power worth wielding, with every other sort of power being invalid and counter-productive?

In the meantime, we might prove its efficacy by doing "everything else" with it in our homes and neighbourhoods!

HAVE you ever been mocked as a daydreamer? I have. Which is why this story of Leonardo appealed to me.

Da Vinci is said to have arrived at an inn where a pig was being roasted on a spit. The artist and inventor sat a long time in front of the fire, watching the servant turn the spit and the smoke go up the chimney.

"Tiring work?" he asked the servant. "I imagine you would like a rest."

"I would, sir. But who, then, would turn the spit?"

Leonardo might have taken the boy's place. Instead, he muttered "the smoke" and left.

He returned some time later with gears and a fan. When it was all in place, the smoke – the rising hot air – turned the fan, which turned the gears, which turned the spit.

Daydreamers look like they are doing nothing. Often, they are thinking of a better world. And, sometimes, they are figuring out how to make that better world come about!

EACH little cut-out, shaped like a man or a woman, had the name of a church member on it.

We were invited to write what we thought of the person, or what they represented in the church, on the little card shapes.

I loved what people wrote about the Lady of the House, but I was reluctant to look at mine.

You see, I knew I might go one of two ways. I might get conceited if the comments were good, or start asking myself why they weren't better.

So, when a five-year-old friend of ours asked if he could have my little card figure to draw a face on and colour in, it seemed like the best conclusion.

Then I started wondering. Was that humility? I'm excellent at humility – did anyone write *humility* on my card?

I did notice that no-one said "Christ-like", or "perfect", and so the journey, and the learning, continues.

Monday — June 14

HAVE you heard of the First Fight Box?
When people get married, they do so with the best of intentions. Their hopes are high and they would do anything for each other.

That doesn't always last. So, in anticipation of that – perhaps inevitable – first fall-out, some couples prepare a box with reminders of the first flush of their love. Perhaps a copy of their wedding vows, pictures of the happy day, or other personal tokens.

The box gets opened in difficult times as a reminder of what their marriage was intended to be. Hopefully it gets them back on track.

Being reminded of your highest hopes and best intentions is surely a helpful thing, not just in a marriage but in so many aspects of life.

Tuesday — June 15

THE three-year-old was being questioned by a neighbour in the presence of her grandparents. It seemed an impossible question, given the circumstances, but the answer she gave was quite emphatic.

"I love Grampa the most!"

This was immediately followed by, "And I love Grandma more than that!"

The neighbour laughed, the grandparents both seemed more than satisfied with their lot, and I walked on thinking I had just seen a fine diplomat in the making.

Wednesday — June 16

RIVERS meander. For the people who live alongside them it must seem like they always existed in their familiar course, but weather and geological conditions almost inevitably mean that most rivers have flowed in a dazzling variety of paths.

Some so-called "primitive" societies learned literally to "go with the flow". Much as we might like the security of the familiar in life, and as difficult as change might be, everything changes. It comes with life's territory.

Don't stay in the one place, physically or emotionally, for ever. Allow yourself a little meander from time to time.

River Oykel and Oykel Bridge, Scottish Highlands.

The meandering river follows its own path.

AN old Italian tale has a wealthy man walking the highway and spying another man, clothed in rags, walking towards him. He took a tighter hold on his purse and looked around for escape routes, in case the man tried to rob him.

As they drew nearer, he realised the malnourished man would not have the strength to overpower him, but no doubt, he would spin some tale of woe. So the wealthy man prepared to harden his heart.

At last, they met, eye to eye. The poor man stretched out his hand.

"Do yourself a kindness, sir."

Friday — June 18

THE penmanship was precise. The name and address were complete. The date was added at the bottom. Above it all, was written "Please return this book to".

What should we make of that? Perhaps that the original owner was a pedantic sort, who expected all his possessions to be accounted for. Or, perhaps that he knew he would be sharing his volumes liberally and hoped to enable them, some day, to return.

Given that the date inscribed was 1911, we can't ask him. It could have meant either of those things.

How much better to give him, and each other, the benefit of the doubt.

Saturday — June 19

THERE'S a legend that has the composer George Frideric Handel fighting a duel.

As the men – both composers – took a few practice swings of their swords, Handel stuffed a musical score inside his shirt.

The other composer might have killed him, but the score stopped the point of his blade.

If you look at it one way, that's cheating!

I prefer to see it as keeping what matters most to you close to your heart.

Doing so helps save you from the hurts of the world.

Sunday — June 20

HE was on his way to beg on a busy city-centre street. He seemed to have a host of physical problems and I knew not what psychological issues. As he neared his pitch, dragging one foot and leaning heavily on a stick, he took out the cardboard coffee cup he hoped coins would be dropped into.

Doing this, he realised he also had a pocketful of rubbish. With some effort and one slow step after another, he deviated from the quickest and easiest course so he could drop this litter in a bin.

That's when I saw what I hadn't noticed before. His dignity. A tiny moment that made a difference to my understanding of the man.

This was something he didn't have to do, something that cost him much more effort than it might the rest of us. And yet, he did it.

I understood the wisdom in the words "judge not". I wondered what God, who knew the workings of his soul, saw, and I began to understand better how He can love us in all of our conditions.

Monday — June 21

THE term "Pyrrhic victory" comes from King Pyrrhus, a Greek ruler who battled with the Romans. Despite being victorious in one epic encounter, his losses were so great he might have been better off defeated.

The same king, they say, told a friend he planned to invade Italy.

"What will you do after that?" the friend asked.

"Then I shall conquer France!" Pyrrhus responded.

"And what then?"

"Why, then it will be Germany. And after that I shall conquer Spain!"

"And when you have conquered the whole world," the friend asked, "what shall you do then?"

"Then I shall see out my years at home in contented security."

"It seems to me," the friend said, "that you might do that anyway, without ever leaving your own land."

Unless they are in defence of loved ones, so many of our battles and victories might count as "Pyrrhic", and the world would be better for their absence.

Tuesday — June 22

T is an interesting fact (I hope) that tigers, despite being "big cats", cannot purr. Instead, they express happiness by closing their eyes.

In a world of prey and hunters, closing your eyes signifies incredible trust. It makes you immediately vulnerable. How comfortable would a tiger have to be to do that?

And how blessed are we to have people we can drop our guard with; people we can be vulnerable with and trust to keep us safe?

The very thought is enough to make me purr!

Wednesday — June 23

*A**ND** where the breeze across the valley drifts,*
And summertime is swathed in golden haze,
All blessings flow from God, whose season's gifts,
Blend mellow warmth with sunbeams' streamlined rays.
By meadow's turf, as velvet to the tread,
And trees – whose boughs in laden leaf now shade
An avenue of lace-like greenery, spread
To bring the coolness of a peaceful glade.
Where fragrant blossoms spill upon the air,
For summer's joys are there for all to share.

Elizabeth Gozney

Thursday — June 24

OLD wisdom tells us we can light a thousand candles from one candle, and that first candle will lose none of its radiance.

The poet Alexander Pope had a similar philosophy regarding friends.

"My friendships are increased by new ones," he wrote, "yet no part of the warmth I felt for the old is diminished!"

Here's to friends, new and old.

Some wise but anonymous person once wrote the following lines:

Make new friends but keep the old.
One is silver,
The other gold.

Friday — June 25

I THINK we probably all know the phrase, "A friend in need is a friend indeed". But where did it come from?

I wonder if it was this verse from Richard Barnfield, a friend of William Shakespeare:

He that is thy friend indeed, he will help thee in thy need.
If thou sorrow, he will weep. If thou wake, he cannot sleep.
Thus, of every grief in heart, he with thee doth bear a part.
These are certain signs to know faithful friend from flatt'ring foe.

Saturday — June 26

T HOMAS MOORE was famed as a singer and poet when, around 1850, he visited the Dublin grocer shop where he grew up.

Later that day, he was guest of honour at the Lord-Lieutenant's Palace and servants carved his meat. But the shop visit made a bigger impression.

Not only was it the home of his childhood, but the grocer took great delight in showing him the bedrooms, the garrets and the little dark kitchen.

As Moore described it, "he entered at once into my feelings".

What a lovely expression!

What greater kindness or tribute could we ever show another person than to enter into their feelings?

Sunday — June 27

I FOUND myself beside a woman I didn't recognise at the charity shop till.

"That's a beautiful christening dress you're buying. Who's it for?"

"I don't know yet," she told me. "I'm here on holiday. Back home there are a lot of people who don't have anything as nice as this.

"So, I'll take it back with me, and when I hear of a child getting christened . . ."

She doesn't yet know who that child will be and neither do I. But I do know one thing.

She will be starting her life wrapped in God's loving provision.

Monday — June 28

*I LOVE to see a sunset that transforms the evening sky
With orange, purple, yellow; gorgeous hues that please the eye.
They fill me with such gratitude at nature's gifted hand,
As day meets night I'll happily admire them as I stand.
To me a perfect sunset is creation at its best
To see one is a privilege – a reminder to feel blessed,
And so I will continue to admire each wondrous view
And revel in these sunsets – sent from heaven – as I do.*

Judy Jarvie

Tuesday — June 29

A WISE man from the east once said, "Just as the body is purified by water, the mind is purified by learning, the heart is purified by love, and the self is purified by tears."

I may not share the gentleman's history or faith, but I can still recognise the wisdom in his words.

And I, too, have felt the benefit of a drink of water, been restored by a good book, been renewed by love, and refreshed – purified, if you like – by a good cry!

Wednesday — June 30

THE scientist Emanuel Swedenborg dreamed he was walking in Heaven.

Coming to a field where sports and games were being played by angels, he was surprised to see that those in charge looked like children.

An adult angel explained.

"Those that you take to be children are really the oldest and wisest amongst us.

"You must know that to grow old in Heaven is to grow young: for the angels of Heaven are always advancing towards the spring-time of their youth."

After reading this, I put the book down and said a heartfelt thank-you for those I know who are already doing this fine work – behind their wrinkles and grey hairs.

July

ADA LOUISE HUXTABLE, the American architect and critic, wrote about this time of the year: "Summer is the time when one sheds one's tensions with the world, and the right kind of day is jewelled balm for the battered spirit. A few of those days and you can become drunk with the belief that all's right with the world."

As a Pulitzer-Prize-winning writer, Ms Huxtable might be considered to know what she was talking about. But if it is not too presumptuous, perhaps you will bear with me while I add two points.

Firstly, may this summer have enough days like that to convince you that all is, in fact, well with the world. Secondly, may I wish us the shedding of those tensions anyway. Leave them aside long enough to breathe, to relax, to see the beauty that surrounds us – and we might never pick them up again!

Ah, summer! It's good for what ails us.

IN days when abandoned women and children could live "off the parish", the church wardens would sometimes search for the runaway husband and bring him back.

When King George II was too long away from England, a notice was posted on the gate of St James's Palace.

It read, *Lost or strayed out of this house, a man who has left a wife and six children on the parish. Whoever will give tidings of him to the church wardens shall receive four shillings and sixpence reward. This reward will not be increased, nobody judging him to be deserving of a crown.*

A crown was, of course, five shillings (a lot of money in the 1700s), and also something a worthy ruler might wear.

Be we man or woman, let us always bear our responsibilities so that we be worthy of a crown – whichever meaning we attach to the word!

Saturday — July 3

HOW much does it take to make someone happy? Not much. But such little effort surely only produces a fleeting effect.

Sydney Smith, the 18th- and 19th-century English preacher, thought otherwise.

"Mankind is always happier for having been happy. So that if you make them happy now, you make them happy twenty years hence – by the memory of it."

I remembered having read that in a book many years ago. It made me smile then – and it still does today. On a more serious note, if any of us ever needed some encouragement to spread a little happiness, Mr Smith's words are surely just the thing!

Sunday — July 4

GREEK philosopher Aristotle was said to have given alms to a man deemed unworthy.

Perhaps called upon to explain himself, Aristotle defended the action rather than the man.

"I did give," he said, "but it was to mankind."

Like Aristotle's friends, we probably spend far too much time deciding who is worthy and who is unworthy of our help. But, as the great man pointed out, we are all mankind. If we help one of God's children, we help the whole family.

Monday — July 5

SIR WALTER SCOTT was visiting Ireland when an elderly woman offered to sell him some gooseberries. Perhaps he had recently dined, for he passed her by.

When, a few yards further on, Sir Walter's daughter gave some coins to a beggar, the woman shouted that they might just as well have helped her, because she was an "old struggler".

The great romantic writer turned around and gave her some money, declaring that "old struggler" ought to be a title of distinction, indicating as it did someone who had never given up.

Here's to those with the title of struggler, whatever age they be.

Be mindful of those we may meet on life's path.

Cliffs of Moher, Ireland.

Tuesday — July 6

IN the last years of the 19th century, the Reverend Charles Little compiled two substantial books of quotes: Biblical Lights and Historical Lights.

The "lights" for him were the people or the words that lifted the experience of life above the ordinary.

For some, though, those lights (being hundreds of years old) might seem beautiful while being as distant as stars.

There are no lights quite like the lights of home and no place better to make a difference.

Shine where you live, and where your loved ones are.

Wednesday — July 7

IT is said that when Napoleon the First was crossing the Alps to fight the armies of England and Austria, he fell to talking with their guide.

The guide, unaware of his companion's rank, spoke of his home and the girl he loved but was too poor to marry.

At the end of the journey and before the battle, Napoleon granted the young man a home fit to take a bride to.

Why am I praising Napoleon?

Because I like to think that none of us – Emperor or otherwise – would be so busy we would walk past a chance to do a little good on the way.

Thursday — July 8

THE Ainu are an indigenous people living in Japan and Russia. Those modern cultures have all but destroyed the Ainu ways. Their language – which has no written version – is believed to be spoken only by a very few, usually very old, people.

Why am I mentioning it?

Because I read that the Ainu language has no words with which one person might abuse or denigrate another.

Something worth preserving?

And something worth emulating?

Friday — July 9

I **MENTIONED** one family's dire situation to a friend who lived a comfortable life. Seemingly without thinking about it, he said he would help.

Relieved, I said I would tell them first thing in the morning. It was late, after all.

Then he surprised me.

"No," he said. "Tell them tonight, if you possibly can. They won't mind when they discover what you have to say. And you will spare them another night of worry."

I knew then he had thought deeply about his gift, and given it with grace.

Saturday — July 10

AN Indian tour guide shared the story of his parents' romance with a friendly tourist.

"Beautiful," the tourist said. "I wish I could find a love like that."

The guide waved at the temple they were about to visit.

"How many of these beautiful, intricate, inspiring structures do you think my ancestors found in the jungle? None. They found a spot by fresh water, made a clearing, then started building.

"Love that lasts isn't found. It's built. Don't waste time looking for a mystical temple. Find a clearing where you can drink fresh water with someone.

"Then, if you both wish to stay together . . . then you start building."

Sunday — July 11

HOPEFULLY, there are plenty of flowers around you – especially at this time of year! If not, you could search some out.

They make me think of the Zen saying: "No seed ever sees the flower."

It reminds me of the importance of planning ahead. It also reminds me that the best of our works will always be, as Jesus showed, the sacrifices we make for the sake of others.

Monday — July 12

IN the year 1685, James Salter was fined five pounds for letting a stretch of river he was responsible for fall into "ruination".

Doubtless, he made the money back when he opened his "coffee-and-curiosities" shop.

The treasures from far-flung places that attracted his clientele included beads made from the bones of St Anthony of Padua, relics from Troy, some of Job's tears, and a block of Solomon's Temple.

Those items may or may not have been genuine (and I'm pretty sure they weren't), but it's a thought that they attracted more people than the river itself.

When more and more are at risk of "ruination", perhaps it is time we started seeing an unspoiled river as a treasure in its own right.

If you can, make time today to appreciate a genuine treasure.

Tuesday — July 13

NICOLA showed me a picture on her phone of her three-year-old daughter, Evie. Her worried but defiant little face was covered in make-up – as was the window behind her!

"Ohhhh!" I exclaimed. "How angry were you?"

"A little," she responded. "But that was swept away by the lesson."

I had to ask, and she explained.

"The lesson is that she watches me and tries to be like me. If she's going to do as I do, that's an encouragement to do better.

"And then," Nicola added, "I showed her how I clean windows!"

Wednesday — July 14

I AM no student of American history, but I am sure President Theodore Roosevelt did many great things for his country.

After a hunting incident his name, shortened to Teddy, became associated with a bear cub, giving rise to the notion of a teddy bear.

I wonder how many children have, since then, gone to sleep comforted by their own teddy bear. And I wonder if that isn't a greater legacy than any man or woman in power ever had.

Watch and you will learn.

Shutterstock.

Thursday — July 15

MY neighbour was doing a kitchen renovation. Hearing he was going to take a ceiling down, I sympathised.

"That's always a messy job!"

He agreed, but seemed distracted. I asked what he was thinking.

"I redid the bathroom above the kitchen a while back. I had some of the floorboards up to fix the pipes. And all the rubbish – the offcuts, the sawdust, the general mess – I swept between the rafters and hid it under the floorboards.

"So I know exactly what's coming down on my head when I take the ceiling down. Because I put it there myself!"

Tidy up as you go along. Our mums told us that for good reason!

Friday — July 16

WERE you ever accused of wool-gathering (daydreaming) as a child? I know I was!

Wool-gathering used to be a part of country life. People too poor to have their own sheep would collect tufts of wool they found on bushes, brambles or fences. Enough tufts might eventually turn into a hat or pullover.

But because it often took ages to find very much, it looked to the casual observer like the wool-gatherer was simply wandering.

Making something out of nothing: that's what wool-gatherers did, and what children with good imaginations still do!

Saturday — July 17

IT warms my heart every time I see it. Flashing blue lights appear on the road and drivers will, as one, slow and pull over to the sides of the road, leaving a clear path for the ambulance or fire engine.

The various demands on their time are momentarily set aside to help someone they will probably never meet. And there is always the thought that, should they ever need the emergency services, others will let them through.

There is a selflessness and yet a connectedness in those times that reassures me there is hope for humanity.

WHAT makes a good human being? Philosophers have debated this across the ages. They have come up with such a wide variety of answers that their efforts have become meaningless.

Marcus Aurelius, who was described as the last of the good Roman Emperors, gave advice that went to the heart of the matter – advice we might all profit from today.

"Waste no more time arguing about what a good human being should be. Be one."

The same might apply to faith. There are so many denominations and interpretations that we might spend (or waste) a lifetime studying them.

How about we simply take the teachings of Christ and the examples of the disciples, however they come to us, and live them?

The world will surely be a better place for our efforts.

THERE is a legend in the French city of Marseille of a man named Guyot who lived there back when the city was a town.

Despite being very wealthy, he was mocked by his neighbours. You see, he dressed in rags and slept on a straw-covered stone floor.

He worked hard, year after year, but spent almost none of his money.

People reckoned him a miser, or insane. They mocked him openly. Children pursued him in the streets.

On his death, his will was made public.

In it Guyot had written how much it had distressed him in his youth to see poor people pay for fresh water, so he dedicated his life to raising enough money to build them an aqueduct.

And that's what happened.

Now, it may be that Guyot was strange – but strange people seldom think themselves so.

In their heads and hearts are often reasons why they are as they are.

In memory of Guyot, we might do them the honour of assuming those reasons are good ones.

*SOMETIMES when the way is tough,
Strength fails, we have had enough,
Tears fall, we cannot go on,
And hope for the future gone.*

*In this time of deep despair,
God's the one who's always there,
He reaches out, drying tears,
Hugging away all our fears.*

*Don't give up. He's by your side
Through this life's chaotic ride;
He'll guide, direct and lead you;
Love and light will get you through.*

Amanda-Jayne Lanceley

Wednesday — July 21

SEVEN years ago, Jim saw a stray cat sniffing about his bins. After asking around for an owner, he started leaving food out. Eventually, the cat (whom he named Hooligan) came into the house to sleep. But he always hid behind the furniture and would not allow himself to be touched by anyone.

This week, however, Hooligan has been settling on his lap.

"Love is sometimes a long haul," Jim tells me, "but it's worth it!"

Thursday — July 22

SHEILA'S friend had been to a concert and messaged her, saying how much she would have loved it. Then she went on.

I typed that, then, as I was walking away from the laptop, I thought, "Of course she would. That's what Sheila does with her life. She loves!"

That's a lovely take on a friend's attitude, but it's more than that.

It's also a question for the rest of us. If people had to describe what they thought we usually did with our lives, what would they say?

Friday — July 23

THE shop was having a closing-down sale. I bought some items at rock-bottom prices to give to a charity the Lady Of The House and I help. I told her what I'd done, expecting a pat on the back for my ingenuity.

She said well done, then she phoned the manager and told him about the children the charity supports. The result was me returning to the shop to collect 16 bags worth of stuff, for free!

People are wonderful if you give them the chance. And my sweetheart assures me I don't do too badly.

Saturday — July 24

A FRIEND saw this sign on a community centre wall:
Some kids are smarter than you. Some kids have cooler clothes than you. Some kids are better at sports than you.

It doesn't matter. You have your thing, too. Be the kid who gets along. Be the kid who is generous.

Be the kid who is happy for others. Be the kid who does the right thing. Be the nice kid!

"That might annoy some people," she told me. "They might say we should swap the word 'kid' with the word 'child'. I say we should swap it with the word "person", because the advice applies to us all!"

Sunday — July 25

IF you have more than you need, then build a longer table," is undoubtedly good advice and encourages sharing.

I am sure John Wesley, the father of Methodism, must have had a table. But it wouldn't have been very well "dressed".

An over-zealous tax man, deciding Wesley must surely have wealth stashed away, asked about his silver.

"I have two silver teaspoons in London," Wesley replied, "and two more in Bristol. This is all the silver I have at the moment.

"And I shall not have more while so many people around me are in want."

A man who preached the Gospel, and also lived it.

Monday — July 26

THE little lad was running about in a busy shopping centre. He tripped and fell.

He raised his head among a sea of legs. People gathered around to help but he ignored them. Before he could wail, he saw his mum.

How? Because she dropped to her knees to be at his level. They hugged and then she lifted him up.

Let's not stay put and reach down to help. Let's not wait for people to raise themselves up. Let's meet them where they are.

Tuesday — July 27

NIGEL'S office is in a converted stately home. As utilitarian as the inside of the building is now, it still has a beautiful chandelier in the hall. Once a year, scaffolding is put in place and the maintenance team climb up to inspect it.

Then Nigel discovered a crank-handle in an old cupboard. In the wall of an alcove in the hall was what seemed to be a rusty metal nut. He put them together and turned. The chandelier lowered gently to the floor.

The man who usually erected the scaffolding wasn't best pleased.

"Our way worked fine," he said.

"But the manufacturer's way worked better," Nigel replied.

I couldn't help but feel there was a life lesson there.

Wednesday — July 28

EDWIN STANTON was Secretary of War under President Abraham Lincoln. After the American Civil War ended, he handed his resignation letter to the President, saying he thought his work there was done.

Lincoln threw the letter on the fire. He hugged Stanton.

"You have been a good friend and a faithful public servant, and it is not for you to decide when those things will no longer be needed here."

Good friends are always needed! And faithful public servants are ever in demand!

A RUSSIAN proverb has a man, travelling on foot, overtaken by a man on horseback.

"How about a lift, brother?" he shouted.

The finely dressed man on the horse looked at the walker's rags.

"Who are you calling brother?" he asked.

Then the clouds opened, drenching them both. They took shelter under a tree. When the sun came out, they hung their outer garments up to dry and lay in a field to let the sunshine warm them.

Resuming their journey, the rider turned to the walker.

"How about a lift, brother?"

"Who are you calling brother?" the walker asked again.

"We were equally soaked by the same rain, and equally dried by the same sun. We are brothers," the rider replied.

And the two men completed their journey – equally.

M ANY a man has complained about his wife "fussing" around the house. I am sure I never do, although the Lady Of The House might erroneously disagree.

I have been reading John Galt's "Annals Of The Parish".

His hero praised his new wife's organisational skills.

"Well may I speak of her with commendation. For she is the bee that makes my honey."

If you have a partner in your life who makes it sweeter by their endeavours, you might forgive them a little fussing.

A MERICAN actor Wendell Pierce talked about growing up in a racially segregated town. He pointed to the concentration of talent that flowered in this poor community.

"We took something ugly and made it beautiful."

That is the only effective thing to do with "ugly" – utterly transform it and make the world a better place in the process.

August

Sunday — August 1

WHEN the man from the Christian charity talked about setting up a food bank, I had reservations. I finally put my fears into words.

"What happens when someone turns up in desperate need and our shelves are empty? What do we say to them?"

"I don't know," he said. "And I don't believe you will ever need to know."

That was several years ago. We took the plunge; now it's run by a large team of volunteers. Many businesses and individuals support it, and despite occasional shortages, the shelves have never been empty. No-one has ever been turned away.

I could not have imagined that, but as someone once said, "There are miracles waiting only for you to believe."

Begin in good faith. Wonders will follow!

Monday — August 2

THE French writer and philosopher Voltaire told how Saladin, "the Conqueror of the East", bequeathed his fortune to the poor, regardless of whether they be Muslim, Christian or otherwise.

His thinking was that we should care less about what people believe and more about what people feel.

Our expectations of the next life might differ. But while we are here, we all feel hunger, satisfaction, fear, comfort, loss, love and so on.

If you want to know whether you should treat a stranger as a brother or a sister, ask if they miss anyone, if they love anyone.

If they ever cried at night; if joy makes them laugh.

Then, in sympathy with all the feelings we have in common, understand that we are not so very different after all.

We always get back more than we give.

Tuesday — August 3

KING JOHN (the Good) of France was taken hostage by the English after the battle of Poitiers in 1356. He was released on the promise of a large ransom. But when the French nobles failed to come up with the ransom money, John gave himself back into captivity.

He said, "If good faith should be totally forgotten by the rest of mankind, it ought still to find a place in the breast of princes."

I would dare to qualify that a little and say that if the rest of the world lost faith in honesty and decency, I would hope it might still be found in your breast and in mine!

Wednesday — August 4

IN younger years, there's no denying it, Jane messed up. But she worked hard to rebuild her life and repair broken relationships.

Now, she's a grandmother. She showed me a photo of her hugging her three-year-old grandson.

"Do you know what grandchildren are, Francis?"

Before I could even decide where to start, she continued.

"They are God's way of redeeming you for being an imperfect parent."

I looked again at the photo and, yes, there was a thing divine in it.

Thursday — August 5

JOHN TUNNELL was a Virginian Methodist preacher in the mid-1700s.

It is said that Tunnell, "One of the celebrities of the first conference west of the Alleghanies", had an exceedingly pale complexion.

So much so that one listener declared he had heard a man speak who looked and sounded like he had surely died, gone to Heaven, then come back to tell us how wonderful it was!

No matter how pale or ruddy our complexion, if we have faith we ought to live it in such a way that people think we surely must be good friends with God, and may even have visited His house.

WONDERFUL things often grow from humble beginnings. Hans was the grandson of an immigrant and son of a shoemaker. He went to school, helped his mother with the chores and spent time with his grandmother.

She was a gardener in what we once would have called a poorhouse, or a workhouse. There, widows and widowers with no other means of support would work spinning wheels for their keep.

Young Hans charmed them and listened attentively while they talked of times and places he could never imagine.

Who's to say those rooms, considered shameful by many, were where Hans Christian Andersen learned the value and magic of a good tale? But who's to say they weren't?

DO your circumstances, your finances, your family situation or your location make you think you can't be of much help in the world?

Supposing I said you might equal angels in the doing-good stakes? Would you believe me?

In the poem "Night-Thoughts", written in 1742, Edward Young wrote, "Who does the best his circumstance allow, does well, acts nobly; angels could do no more!"

Defy the limitations of your surroundings. Rise up. Reach for the better. Show the angels how it is done.

AFTER the Battle of Wagram on the banks of the Danube, Napoleon was told of the death of an officer he'd previously had cross words with.

"I regret not having been able to speak with him before the battle, to tell him that I had long ago forgiven everything," he said.

Do you have an apology to make or forgiveness to offer?

Forgiveness and repentance. They are central to our faith for good reason.

And today is always the best day.

Monday — August 9

WHEN Britain was at war with Napoleon the First, an English soldier was found trying to launch a raft made of branches into the Channel.

Visiting him in jail, Napoleon declared the soldier must have been mad to take to sea on such a flimsy craft. Or the woman he was trying to get home to must have been very beautiful!

"She is my mother," the soldier replied. "She is old. She is infirm. And she is very beautiful to me."

Napoleon, so the story goes, sent the soldier home on a French ship under a flag of truce.

With a purse of gold for his mother.

Tuesday — August 10

IT is with shame that I admit I have a talent for arguing. I have, in younger years, won arguments despite knowing I was in the wrong.

What changed me? A line from Socrates.

"If you continue to take delight in idle argumentation, you may be qualified to combat with the sophists, but will never know how to live with men."

Would I rather love than be right? I think I would. It's an ideal worth aspiring to.

Please don't try to argue me out of it.

Wednesday — August 11

I HAVE long believed that the wisest words are often the simplest. In "The Learned Boy", a poem by the surgeon and poet George Crabbe, Stephen is a child raised by a widowed farmer.

When he reaches an age to go off to the city and try to make his fortune, his worried father gives him lots of advice.

To himself, Stephen summarised it this way:

"'Twas good advice, and meant, 'My son . . . be good!'"

Surely the distillation of all the advice ever given by a parent to their child.

Thursday — August 12

DO you ever describe anyone as fifty, sixty or seventy years young, instead of how many years old?

Julia Ward Howe lived a long and full life. She wrote "The Battle Hymn Of The Republic". She was an abolitionist, and may also have inspired that description.

In 1889, Oliver Wendell Holmes wrote this of her: "To be seventy years young is sometimes far more cheerful and hopeful than to be forty years old."

Mrs Howe was hopeful, cheerful and young for a long time afterwards. May we all remember to be so!

Friday — August 13

THE Brahmani were a school of Persian philosophers in the time of Alexander the Great. It is said that, at the evening meal, masters and students were required to recite the good they had done that day. If they had nothing to offer, they did not eat.

A little strict, perhaps. It begs the question of why those with meals didn't add to their goodness by feeding those who went without.

I guess it was an encouragement. I hope they reached the point where kindness became as essential to their lives as breathing – before they became too skinny!

Saturday — August 14

LYCURGUS was the (perhaps real, perhaps mythical) law-giver of Ancient Sparta. The rules and regulations governing discipline, training and warfare are said to stem from him.

It is said that, in each of the training halls, he insisted there be a little god of laughter.

The Spartans grew famous for their austerity. So much so that the word "spartan" has come to suggest "no frills". Who knew laughter was such an important part of that strict regimen?

When it seems that work – or anything else – has overtaken your weekend, find a little space in there for laughter.

If it was good enough for the Spartans . . .

Sunday — August 15

IN his novel, "The Land Of Long Lost Friends", Alexander McCall Smith wrote, "Ask anybody what their idea of heaven is, and the answer will reveal that person's soul."

So I asked around.

A wide range of answers included opera, the company of children, the shoreline, dogs, teamwork, beautiful skies, snuggling in front of a fire, good books and being loved.

I didn't do much soul analysing – they were friends, after all – but I was left with the distinct impression that Heaven must be endlessly variable. And it might just be all around us!

Monday — August 16

DO you ever feel insignificant, and that your efforts aren't worth, well, the effort? Or that nothing you do makes a difference?

Samuel Johnson, the great lexicographer, wrote, "Pound St Paul's Cathedral into atoms and consider any single atom. It is, to be sure, good for nothing. But put all these atoms together and you have St Paul's Cathedral."

Little things have unexpected importance. For without little things we would have no great things.

Put your little effort to good use.

Tuesday — August 17

BESSIE ANDERSON STANLEY doesn't always get credited with writing the poem "Success", which contains these lines:

"He achieved success who has lived well, laughed often, and loved much; who has enjoyed the trust of pure women, the respect of intelligent men and the love of little children."

Such profundity is often (wrongly) attributed to the likes of Ralph Waldo Emerson or Robert Louis Stevenson.

Now we know the truth. Bessie Anderson Stanley wrote it for a competition in 1904, won $250, and left a beautiful legacy for the world to enjoy.

I'd say Mrs Stanley was a good definition of success herself.

ONCE upon a summertime
When all the world was young,
The sunlight filled each happy day
As cheerful songs were sung.

All life was an adventure then,
Designed for me and you,
With every day a bright new start.
Do you remember, too?

Can we recapture wonderment
The way it used to be?
The world is still as beautiful;
Let's look around and see.

Once upon a summertime –
Perhaps the time is right
To look for hope and joy and love,
Reach out to life and light.

Iris Hesselden

IT was Caroline's first garden.

So she decided she would grow a pretty flower border along her fence.

The plants were doing well until her four-year-old son and the boy next door discovered a loose fence slat.

They used it as a shortcut between the gardens.

Of course, the flowers got trampled.

So Caroline planted mint there.

Now, every time the mint gets stood on, the garden smells beautiful.

Oliver Goldsmith put it like this in his poem "The Captivity":

"Aromatic plants bestow no spicy fragrance while they grow

But crushed or trodden to the ground, diffuse their balmy sweets around."

Is there anywhere more relaxing than a garden?

Friday — August 20

I WOULD have done, but . . ."
I know a lot of nice people with good hearts who wish they could do more, but shyness, fear or any number of other reasons stop them stepping out in kindness.

I wish they could know the feeling that follows the overcoming of those inhibitions.

James Russell Lowell, one of the "Fireside Poets", wrote this: "Every man feels instinctively that all the beautiful sentiments in the world weigh less than a single lovely action."

Saturday — August 21

L OVE one another." It has to be the best way to do the maximum good for the most people.

And yet it's a lot to ask, isn't it? Love everyone? Some people just don't seem very loveable.

How about, if we can't do all of that all at once, we move towards it in smaller steps?

In the novel "Daniel Deronda", George Eliot wrote: "Affection is the broadest basis for good in this life."

Affection, then – can we manage that?

Show the world and its inhabitants enough affection and love will grow.

Both ways.

Sunday — August 22

*IT'S just a little garden, but on such days as this
Even little gardens can be a place of bliss:
The joyful trill of songbirds, the hum of busy bees,
The sight of currants ripening, the taste of fresh-picked peas.
The hollyhocks and roses, the scents of every bloom,
The sunlight in the courtyard that warms away all gloom.
To see so much to please one, within this tiny space –
It's time to fetch the deckchair, for here's the perfect place!*

Maggie Ingall

Monday — August 23

WHEN his father died, young Matthew Prior acquired the patronage of the Earl of Dorset. In appreciation, he sent the Earl a lengthy poem each year.

In one, he referred to the political and religious factions around the Earl – this was in the 17th century.

There was a sure and simple path through those complications which he complimented his benefactor on always taking.

"One single positive weighs more, you know, than negatives by the score."

Tuesday — August 24

JOHN NEWTON, who wrote "Amazing Grace", had a great zeal for doing good.

And when he couldn't, he did some "rebalancing".

If he found a penny a child had dropped and he couldn't find that child, then that child would be sad.

If Newton stopped there, the accumulated misery of the world would be larger by a penny-worth.

On the other hand, if he gave that penny to a child who needed it, that child's happiness might counteract the other's sadness in some cosmic scale.

Perhaps we might all keep an eye on that balance, and do our bit to make sure it keeps tilting in favour of the good.

Wednesday — August 25

BORN in 1883, Mary Abigail Dodge lived in a time when women lived quite restricted lives and had limited opportunities.

Despite that, she worked for the abolition of slavery and, as a governess, helped shape the lives of the children in her charge.

"Every person is responsible for all the good within the scope of their abilities. And none can tell whose sphere of influence is the largest."

Limitations are, sometimes, for some souls, nothing more than a more enticing challenge.

Thursday — August 26

AN entry in Great-aunt Louisa's diary read, "My attention was caught by a pile of dusty almanacs on a shelf. Doubtless, they were full of useful dates, interesting facts and humorous stories, but they were from years gone by. And so, those who hadn't already read them paid them no heed."

Then I read this line by Cato.

"The best way to keep good acts in memory is to refresh them with the new."

Enjoy tales of good deeds done previously. Honour them by doing likewise today.

Friday — August 27

BEAUTY is easily found in summertime, but does it seem so abundant in the mid-winter? Wonders are easily spotted in exotic places, but how often do we stop and stare admiringly at something in our own neighbourhood?

The Irish writer Felicia Hemans asked similar questions in the poem "Our Daily Paths".

"There's beauty all around our paths," Mrs Hemans wrote, "if but our watchful eyes can trace it 'midst familiar things, and through their lowly disguise."

A challenge, if you like, that we might all enjoy accepting.

Saturday — August 28

WE are all creatures of habit. Some don't appear so because their habits are good ones and we tend only to notice the negative, socially damaging behaviours.

Then we get frustrated and ask, "Why do they have to be that way? Why do they always behave like that?"

Mark Twain had a more charitable approach to the matter.

"Habit is habit," he wrote, "and is not to be thrown out the window by any man, but coaxed downstairs, one step at a time."

Gentle, continuous encouragement has the best hope of turning bad habits good.

It's easy to see the
Creator's hand.

Beautiful Barbados.

116

Sunday — August 29

EMANUEL SWEDENBORG, the 18th-century writer and theologian, had some deeply insightful ideas – and some weird ones. For instance, this great thinker thought the Last Judgment had happened in 1757, the year before he wrote about it.

But there was nothing odd about his "Rules of Life"!

- Often read and meditate upon the Word of God
- Submit everything to Divine Providence
- Observe in everything a propriety of behaviour that will keep the conscience clear
- Discharge with fidelity the functions of my employment
- And render myself, in all things, useful to society.

Monday — August 30

THOMAS CARLYLE was not afraid of addressing great matters of state in his essay collection "Signs Of The Times".

How did he suggest we dealt with them? He didn't.

"Our grand business," he wrote, "undoubtedly, is not to see what lies dimly at a distance, but to do what lies clearly at hand."

Many think, rightly I am sure, that big issues do need to be taken in hand. But let's not forget the difference that can be made on our own doorsteps.

Tuesday — August 31

THERE was an early morning mist. If there hadn't been, I might not have noticed the spiderweb strung between the gate and the garden shed. It looked like it was bedecked by diamonds.

I was reluctant to open the gate, but I needed to go out.

As the gate opened, I saw the web sag. As it sagged, the mist clinging there gathered into larger droplets.

They ran together to the bottom strands, then they fell to the grass.

The web seemed to rebound, being free of the weight.

By being flexible, it lightened its own load.

September

SUMMER was wonderful. But all good things come to an end. Actually, I'm not a big fan of that expression. The fact that good things come to an end ignores the fact that other good things almost always arrive in their place.

The move from summer to autumn happens this month. We leave one beautiful season behind and transition seamlessly into one no less wonderful.

George Arnold, a New Jersey-born portrait-painter turned poet, seemed to have a real preference for this time of the year.

"O, sweet September, thy first breezes bring the dry leaf's rustle and the squirrel's laughter.

"The cool fresh air where health and vigour spring. And promise of exceeding joy hereafter!"

SIR WALTER SCOTT was walking with his friend Mr Morritt. After a while, Sir Walter confessed that he had taken Morritt quite some distance only to see a cottage which was nothing much to look at – but which he could not pass.

It was the first home he and his wife lived in together, a place they had worked hard to make habitable.

He pointed out the willow trees at either side of the gate. He had tied them together to make a sort of archway. A rough cross he made from two pieces of wood could still be seen in their branches.

"To be sure, it isn't much to show a stranger," the great author said. "But after I had constructed it, Mrs Scott and I thought it so fine we turned out to see it by moonlight and walked backwards from it to the cottage door."

Our achievements in this world needn't be grand to be special. They simply need to be done in a spirit of love.

Friday — September 3

DOING a little self-examination, Jim wondered if he helped people – and he helps many – for selfish reasons. Encouragement and praise hadn't been a part of his growing up. He wondered if his drive to do good was actually a quest for praise.

"If that turned out true," I asked, "would you behave differently?"

"No!"

I shared with him a line from a poem where Oliver Goldsmith describes a character as being flawed but "E'en his failings lean'd to virtue's side."

We are all imperfect beings, but so long as our flaws are put to the good of others, then they might even be called virtues.

Saturday — September 4

WHY must we go through trying times?
I am sure you have heard about the process for refining gold. The raw materials are heated over a flame, in a crucible. As it boils, everything that isn't gold rises to the surface, where it is disposed of. What's left is the best of it.

Sir Lewis Morris, the Welsh academic and poet, in his poem "Comfort" wrote of a similar process.

"From out the throng and stress of lies, From out the painful noise of sighs, One voice of comfort seems to rise: "It is the meanest part that dies."

Why must we go through trying times? So that we can be better because of them.

Sunday — September 5

SHE has a funny way of joking, does our friend Mary.
I knew for sure it wasn't her birthday, so I was a little puzzled when she told me she'd opened two wonderful gifts that morning.

"Gifts from God, Francis," she explained. "My eyes! They enable me to see that confused look on your handsome face!"

Like I said, a funny way of joking . . . while reminding me of my blessings.

I SEE the season changing as I walk along the street,
Crisp, coppery leaves begin to fall and tumble at my feet,
Their orange, brown and berry shades – in glorious autumn blaze –
Lift my spirit as we say farewell to warmer summer days.

Afternoons are mellow and turn golden in the sun,
Lamplight bids me welcome when the autumn days are done,
And when I close the curtains against the evening gloom,
A warm fire burns so cheerfully within my cosy room.

Although the winter lies ahead, I have God's truth to hold,
His radiant love to fire my soul although the world is cold,
So I will rest on faith whenever life is grey and drear –
Inside the prayer room of my heart, God is always near.

                                                    Marian Cleworth

WATER! We complain when it falls from the sky, we walk carefully when it freezes, we appreciate it in a nice warm bath or shower. It's a refreshing drink. It is also the first thing scientists look for when they are searching for life on other planets.

Its importance cannot be overstated, but there are also aspects of it better described by poets and mystics than by scientists. The Persian philosopher Rumi said, "Wherever water flows, life flourishes. Wherever tears fall, divine mercy appears."

HOW do you choose your friends? I imagine that for most of us, acquiring new friends is simply something that happens.

Jeremy Taylor, the Poet of the Divines, was more practical.

"When I choose a friend, I choose such a one that can do me many kindnesses if I need them."

By "kindnesses" he didn't mean a borrowed cup of sugar or a hand with the DIY. He meant such kindnesses as "make me wiser and make me better."

Friends should encourage the best in us.

Thursday — September 9

THOSE of us going through difficult times sometimes take comfort in the notion that it is often darkest before the dawn. But perhaps we don't take enough. There is nothing surer than that the dawn will come.

In 1843, in his poem "Orion", Richard Hengist Horne wrote: "It is always morning, somewhere in the world."

And the sun has risen, the dawn has arrived, every day since then!

A new day will happen, and our current afflictions will be left with the old.

Friday — September 10

MAY it never be said I am one of those who sacrifice the present day to the memory of some idyllic past. That being said, previous ages seemed to hold manners in higher esteem.

Of course, sometimes there was too much emphasis on them at the cost of sincerity.

These days, we seem busy to a point where such fineries fall by the wayside.

Ralph Waldo Emerson, the American essayist and philosopher, wrote: "Life is not so short (or so busy) but that there is always time for courtesy."

We can easily do something about it, if we will. Shall we? Please?

Saturday — September 11

AS a biographer, Thomas Carlyle was used to seeing the whole person. He believed it a wise approach that before complaining about a person's faults we should count up all the good things about them.

That way, the problem could be seen in a proper perspective.

How might that change outcomes the next time we are annoyed with something someone else does?

Take a minute to see the whole person. Compile a mini-biography of your own.

And then offer your response.

Sunday — September 12

LORD BYRON wrote: "I loathe that low vice – curiosity!" I wonder why he said that. Science, with all its resources and all the centuries of its existence, has not run out of things to discover.

How then, could I be bored with God's creation? The more I know of it, the more I want to know.

The closer I look, the more I find to be curious about.

The gap between my Creator's abilities and my human understanding means I will be curious to the end. Followed by being amazed that it isn't!

Monday — September 13

HOW would you like to explore a warehouse? No? How about if I said you didn't have to leave your chair?

Henry Ward Beecher once described many men as being "warehouses full of merchandise. The head, the heart, are stuffed with merchandise.

"There are apartments in their souls which were once tenanted by taste, and love, and joy, and worship, but they are all deserted now and the rooms are filled with earthly and material things."

Such things can be important at certain times in our lives. But, when we no longer have to give them our whole attention, remember the other rooms. Explore. Refamiliarise yourself with them. Make yourself at home in them again.

Tuesday — September 14

I AM a man on a mission," Harry said, closing his garden gate firmly behind him.

"How so?" I enquired.

"I have been in a good mood for several days now – which you know isn't like me. In fact," he continued, "it is fairly tiring me out!"

"What's a man to do?" I wondered.

"Well, it's too nice a thing to just stop. So, I'm off to pass it on to someone who needs it!"

I wished him all the best on his wonderful mission.

Wednesday — September 15

OUR dear friend lives in an old cul-de-sac. Because it's not accessible to larger vehicles, residents take their wheelie-bins to the car park on collection day.

"There are four different colours of bins. Remembering which one to take out can be tricky.

"Usually, people check to see what their neighbours put out. But this week, the first person got it wrong. They chose the blue instead of the brown.

"Someone else followed suit. The more blue bins there were in the car park, the more people were convinced that was right. In the end, no-one got their bins emptied!"

"That's terrible," I said. Then I waited. And she did not disappoint.

"If that's the difference a bad example can make," she said, "just think what a good example could achieve.

Her words of advice aren't rubbish. And they're recyclable.

Thursday — September 16

WAS he talking about how our earthly lives lead to a more glorious one? Was he talking about how little acts of kindness do more good than we can possible imagine? I didn't know, and I didn't care to find out.

This line from Sir Edwin Arnold's poem "Light Of Asia" had all the possibilities of those two, and enough beauty for an entire poem:

"The dewdrop slips into the shining sea."

Friday — September 17

IT is a frustration of mine that gentleness is often seen as weakness. Those who advocate a more "realistic" response have no idea how much courage it sometimes takes to be gentle. Most often their "practical" approach to such matters is simply an unwillingness to try them, because they fear they might not be up to the task.

But those who choose the nobler virtues gain real comfort and strength to be had there. As Orlando says in Shakespeare's "As You Like It", "Let gentleness my strong enforcement be."

A beautiful
stretch of blue.

Shutterstock.

Llangrannog, Wales.

125

Saturday — September 18

GOSSIP might not be the scourge of society that it once was. Or perhaps I have stopped hearing it around me. God forbid that I no longer hear it because I have starting doing it myself!

But this description of that bad habit by the novelist George Eliot did make me smile.

"Gossip is a sort of smoke that comes from the dirty tobacco-pipes of those who diffuse it: it proves nothing but the bad taste of the smoker."

Sunday — September 19

WORDS that are spelled the same but have different meanings often have common roots. We have "kind" as in "the same kind" and "kind" as in "be kind to one another".

Different meanings. But is it such a stretch to think that if we were of the same kind we would automatically be kind to each other?

Who knows?

It's a thought worth considering, and was inspired by these words from 19th-century English poet Philip James Bailey:

"Both mankind and womankind belie their nature when they are not kind."

Whatever the connection between the words, let us be kind to our kind.

And every man and woman, every boy or girl, is of our kind.

Monday — September 20

YOU may have heard people say, "I'll forgive, but I won't forget." It seems a reasonable defensive measure, but it actually means carrying an unpleasant memory around for the rest of our lives.

The poet Robert Browning's approach to the matter could be summed up in four simple words:

"Good to forgive; best to forget."

Ralph Waldo Emerson described a friend as having a heart "as great as the world" but still with "no room in it to hold the memory of a wrong".

Tuesday — September 21

THE cat had fallen into the pond. The little wall around the pond was too tall for the cat to escape. It clung to the side, getting more and more exhausted.

A dog leaned over the edge. The cat swiped at it. The dog reached in with a paw. The cat scratched it.

The dog jumped into the pond, coming to the surface beneath the cat, which clung on to it with all four sets of claws.

The dog scrambled out of the pond and the cat ran off. Safe.

That is sacrificial love. The cat reacted out of fear. People who are difficult to help will have reasons we might never learn of.

Expect no thanks – but love them anyway!

Wednesday — September 22

HOW do we improve humanity?
Some would do it through laws that curb the worst excesses of people; some through improving the conditions people live in; some through charity and increasing availability of opportunities.

Those are all very well and good. We might also consider the idea of historian and magazine editor James Anthony Froude. In his "Short Studies On Great Subjects", published in 1878, he wrote, "Human improvement is from within – outward!"

Don't worry about correcting others. Be the best you can be. If others follow your example, then all well and good. If not, then at least your part of humanity will be improved.

Thursday — September 23

MANY of the Roman Emperors were known for their excesses and their decadent lifestyles. They were, after all, the most powerful people in the world. Who was going to tell them no?

Marcus Aurelius was a bit more philosophical than the others, and what he realised applies equally to us non-emperor types.

"Whatever anyone else does or says," he wrote, "I must be good."

It's a decision no-one else makes for us. From time to time we must tell *ourselves* no. And be better for it.

Friday — September 24

SIR LAUNFAL was an Arthurian knight put into verse by the American poet James Russell Lowell.

In younger years he was a fine and somewhat haughty knight, but as an older man he found himself in reduced circumstances, with only a crust of bread to his name.

When he encountered a leprous beggar seeking alms, he broke the crust in half and sat with the man so they both might eat. Of course, the beggar was none other than Jesus. He rose.

"Who gives himself with his alms feeds three. Himself, his hungering neighbour, and me."

It's fine to feed the hungry, but to sit with them, to share your love – that's when you know you're giving as Jesus would have it done.

Saturday — September 25

HAVE you ever had to choose between the easy path, Francis," our dear friend Mary asked, "and the right path?"

Before I could speak, she guessed my answer.

"I won't ask which one you chose. But I know a lot of people think the right way too difficult. The thing is, the more you walk a difficult path, the more the brambles get beaten back, the more the nettles get broken down, the more the stones get pushed into the dirt.

"Eventually, what you are left with is a path that's a pleasure to walk – the more so because of the effort you put into it."

Sunday — September 26

WILLIAM COWPER was an 18th-century poet and hymn-writer. It almost goes without saying that he thought deeply about life.

So, what did this wise man suggest was the only remnant of Paradise to survive the Fall?

Domestic bliss. A happy home-life.

Adam and Eve had it in Eden before things went so dreadfully wrong. If we can recreate it in our homes, then we have kept a little bit of paradise in the world.

And that is no small thing!

Find a path that's a pleasure to walk!

Monday — September 27

OF what importance are the little things in life?

Well, Julia Carney, a teacher and writer, had this to say in her 1884 poem "Little Things":

"Little deeds of kindness, little words of love, make our pleasant earth below, like the heaven above."

The first verse of the poem, "Little drops of water, little grains of sand, make the mighty ocean and the pleasant land," was written as part of an impromptu 10-minute exercise while she was a student in a shorthand class.

The completed work went on to become a standard text in Sunday schools across America. It was published numerous times and sung countless times.

Little things are often, against all reasonable expectations, the beginning of much bigger, much more important, things.

Tuesday — September 28

THE Lady of the House and I were helping two young friends move house. The bed frames had already been lifted into the van and I was bagging the quilts and pillows.

Amongst them, I found two threadbare little blankets, one pink and one blue. What some might describe as comforters, or "blankies".

Thinking the children might want them at some point during the move, I threw them on to a long white bag lying on the floor.

A few minutes later I noticed that my sweetheart had stopped. She was staring at the bag and the two blankies.

"That bag has Sarah's wedding dress in it," she said softly. "It was laid there so it wouldn't get wrinkled."

Uh-oh! I was sure I was about to get into trouble.

"That's what she wore as a bride, in order to become a wife, and then to be a mother to two little darlings. Like most mums, she is the source of all comfort to her children.

"And you laid their comforters across the feet of that dress."

Then she kissed me on the cheek.

No, I don't understand it, either.

ISAAC NEWTON was one of the cleverest men who ever lived. But he was a bit of a duffer at school, apparently.

At one point he was bottom in the worst-but-one school class.

Then, despite being physically slight, he got into a fight with a classmate. To everyone's surprise, Isaac won and was lauded by all the other boys.

The next morning, however, he was back at the bottom of the class and the boy he beat was at the top.

Newton decided then that victories of the fists couldn't compete with victories of the mind. He started taking his studies more seriously.

We might, from time to time, find ourselves in conflict with others. Violence is never the answer. The best resolution is surely to know better – and to be better.

LOVE is such a special word,
It casts its meaning wide,
Like walking arm in arm,
With your partner by your side.

A warm and happy smile,
Upon the face of a dear friend
The message in their eyes,
That a beloved pet can send.

The pounding of your heart,
Telling you that he's the one,
The overwhelming feeling
As you hold your newborn son.

A grandchild's tiny hand,
That fits inside yours like a glove,
All of these are wondrous,
And all of them are love.

Linda Brown

October

Friday — October 1

OCTOBER! The Saxons used to call this time of year Winterfylleth. They only had two seasons, winter and summer. In October you can actually feel the approach of winter. The natural world is preparing for hibernation time, when everything snuggles down to snooze through the worst of the cold.

We could follow the example of the natural world by getting organised and making sure those around us are, too. Hibernation is better for animals when they snuggle together. Now, I'm not suggesting we snuggle in with our neighbours, but let's not forget each other this Winterfylleth.

Saturday — October 2

*G*OD'S timing is perfect, so do not despair
*If you're keenly awaiting an answer to prayer,
Just keep on believing – one day you will see
A pattern emerging where none used to be.*

*It may take some time, for although we may feel
Our needs to be urgent, our fears to be real,
God knows what He's doing, He's in full control,
But we see a fraction while He sees the whole.*

*Although you may worry and question His will,
He hasn't forgotten, He's waiting until
The threads can be woven to work for your good,
Shaping your destiny just as they should.*

*So if you've a problem be patient . . . and wait,
His answer will not come too early or late,
Take heart and keep trusting, for He understands . . .
God's timing is perfect – your life's in His hands.*

Marian Cleworth

Sunday — October 3

IN his poem "The Seasons", James Thomson wrote, "Think, oh, grateful think! How good the God of Harvest is to you; who pours abundance over your flowing fields."

In 1730, when the poem appeared, the country had a much closer relationship with the land and its harvest. Even in our more technologically advanced age, we are all still dependent on the bounty of the good earth and its Creator.

Give thanks. Be grateful.

Monday — October 4

DECLUTTERING has become fashionable recently, despite always being a good idea. Some people have become famous selling books and DVDs on how to declutter, thereby adding to it in their own small way!

These "influencers" are often quoted, but the best advice I ever heard on the subject came from my neighbour Harry.

"If you are going to declutter," he said, when we met by the recycle bins, "you might as well start with the really worthless stuff."

"Like?" I asked, adding some warm coats to the collection.

"Like hate," Harry said. "Like anger, regrets and guilt."

He's right. Unless they are inspiring something better in you – bin them!

Tuesday — October 5

IF you think autumn a dismal time of year (some do, I hear), then ask yourself how dismal an evening with your feet up seems after a hard day's work. And if winter seems dead to you, it is only as dead as the good night's sleep that sets you up for the next day.

There is nothing wasted or unnecessary in nature. Everything, somehow, fits some part of the larger plan; everything serves some purpose. And we are part of that Grand Scheme.

Have nothing unnecessary in your life, try to understand and appreciate your ebbs and flows, and in your own way, serve a purpose.

Wednesday — October 6

CONFIDENCE. Profoundness. Love. Those are no small things. And yet, according to the 16th-century philosopher Lao Tzu, a little thing can create each of them. The same little thing, actually.

"Kindness in words creates confidence," he wrote. "Kindness in thinking creates profoundness. And kindness in giving creates love."

If you ask me, it's thinking kind thoughts ourselves that creates the profundity required to give others confidence and help them feel loved. Thinking kind thoughts. Not always easy, but definitely a habit worth acquiring.

Thursday — October 7

THE other ages we have been never really leave us. The Lady of the House had requested a new kitchen door.

As I carried the old one outside, grown-up me had a thought.

"I'll take the hinges and handles off. It can go to the wood-chipper."

Then another voice (he sounded about ten years old) spoke.

"Or, if you lash it to a couple of barrels, it would make a raft!"

He knew nothing of the world, that lad, except how to have fun in it.

And I am glad he is still in touch.

Friday — October 8

A CAPRIOLE is the closest earth-bound animals come to flying. It's when they leap with their front legs tucked into their chest and the back legs stretched out behind them.

This morning, I watched five deer "capriole" across moorland. When I tried to walk the way they had gone, I couldn't. The ground was covered with heather and bramble.

Then I understood. The small hooves of the deer touched down only to take off again. Most of the distance they covered was in the air.

I wondered if we humans might travel better if we focused more on higher things and less on the tangled undergrowth.

Saturday — October 9

"LIFE seems all light and all shade, all happiness and all woe," Adelaide Proctor wrote in her 1861 poem, "Dream-life".

"Which, you ask me, is the real life. Which the dream, the joy, or woe? Hush, my friend, it little matters. And, indeed I never know!"

I suggest that it does matter. And, given that one seems as real as the other, I would say that the real one is the one we make real.

Sunday — October 10

SIR ROGER DE COVERLY was a fictional character created by Joseph Addison. He was a wealthy landowner who, in "Sir Roger On The Bench", declared, "A man's first care should be to avoid the reproaches of his own heart."

It wasn't a view Joseph Addison took seriously, and neither should we. If a thing doesn't feel right, if our heart reproaches us over it, then we should listen. And direct our ways accordingly.

Monday — October 11

WRITER and preacher George MacDonald may have set the bar a little high when he said, "I want to help you grow as beautiful as God meant you to be when he thought of you first."

But consider this. When you were a babe someone looked at you and saw your potential and the possibilities open for you.

Be as beautiful as they thought you were and you won't be very far from Reverend McDonald's expectations at all.

Tuesday — October 12

"TO give alms is nothing," John Ruskin wrote, "unless you give thought also. It is not written, 'Blessed is he that feedeth the poor,' but 'Blessed is he that considereth the poor.' A little thought and a little kindness are often worth more than a great deal of money."

A little time, a kind word or two. Give what you would like to be given, should the roles be reversed.

Wednesday — October 13

THE drawing was called "The Mender Of Broken Hearts". Sadly, I couldn't make out the signature. It showed a man in a workshop, wearing an apron and stitching up a cartoon-style heart.

Another heart lay in a vice, waiting for the glue to dry. Several hearts – being tested for leaks – bobbed in a tin-bath of water.

Light-hearted and fun. But imagine that was a real occupation! Mending broken hearts.

I don't know how we would get paid for it, except in heaven. But wouldn't that be work worth doing? Even once?

Thursday — October 14

LIGHT a little candle that glows among the gloom,
It flickers then it builds in strength, transforms the cold, dim
room.
Outside a storm is raging, in here it's safe and warm;
I light another candle; it's a haven from the storm.
And soon the room grows welcoming, transformed to a snug den,
The power of light and hope renew so hearts are cheered again.
Do you bring light and welcome in all the things you do?
We all should strive to strike a match so others trust in you.
Let friendship be your candle and goodness be your flame;
Let love burn strongly in your life – with kindness as your aim.

Judy Jarvie

Friday — October 15

TOLD Mary a story of someone helping a mother with three young children.

"Oh, that's so lovely!" she said. "You know, in a world where people can be as wonderful as that, why would anyone choose to be anything else?"

I confess, I was stumped for an answer, but the question stayed with me. We don't all have the same resources, but we all have hearts, minds and souls. Kindness and love are within the capabilities of each and every one of us.

Wonderful is always an option. So why choose to be anything else?

Let love burn
strongly in your life.

Saturday — October 16

THE Swedes have a proverb.

"When a blind man carries a lame man, they can both go forward."

I have never forgotten the time I saw that in action.

It was in the town's main street. A man in a wheelchair was being pushed by a blind man.

The man in the chair saw everything because his friend provided the propulsion.

And because he kept up a running commentary, his friend "saw" it all, too.

There's no doubt about it: given that we all have our weaknesses, we are much better together.

Sunday — October 17

THERE is a lovely – but serious – story associated with Sister Sledge's disco hit, "We Are Family", which was released in 1979 and was a huge hit.

Political activist Nelson Mandela was imprisoned on Robben Island for 18 of the 27 years he served behind bars before the fall of apartheid. While there, he got to know his guards.

Sometimes this was a good thing; sometimes not.

One guard always used to bring music on duty with him.

In conversation, they discovered that both the guard and the prisoner liked the song "We Are Family".

They talked about the lyrics and what they represented to them. This, amongst other things, helped them get to know each other better.

Of course, Mandela was still in jail at the time.

The song couldn't change that, but it did change that one relationship.

And therefore, isn't it interesting to think that, once we take away the man-made barriers and the prisons of our own prejudices, once we get to know each other, all we are left with is one inescapable conclusion?

Yes, we really are family.

Monday — October 18

WHAT do you think of when you think of religion? Church? Prayers? Hymns? Boring sermons or something more positive?

The word itself comes from the Latin word *religare*. It means to bind together, in the way broken bones heal. It might also be where we get the word "ligament" from, and ligaments play a major role in holding the various parts of our body together.

Whatever it has come to mean, the original intention was that it would bring good-hearted people together; that it would heal the brokenness in the world, and support the body that is mankind.

Tuesday — October 19

CAROLINE has a collection of "historic" photographs. Her favourite is one of a bride-to-be leaving home on her father's arm. Nice, but not special by itself.

What makes it special is that the photo was taken during World War II and the bride's home has been shattered by a bomb.

Yet she looks delighted, her father looks proud, and her mother, with a bouquet of flowers in her arms, is waving happily from a glassless window.

What might have been a scene of despair is one of delight.

"Proof, if it were needed," Caroline told me, "that our situation is never the defining factor in our happiness. But our attitude towards that situation always is."

Wednesday — October 20

HE was selling hot food in the town centre on a cold day. "How's it going?" I asked him.

"Life?" he asked, grinning widely. "It's all good!"

"You look like a man with no troubles," I offered.

"Do I?" he replied. "Well, everyone has troubles. I don't know. Maybe I just wear mine with a little more style."

The food I took away warmed my stomach. But the idea that we have a choice in how we wear our troubles, and that we might wear them with style . . . that warmed my heart!

Thursday — October 21

SOME people are quite prone to repeating what they hear. I am as guilty as anyone of that. Often, as if to make their recitation more interesting, people will add "details" which are nothing more than suppositions and were never there in the original version. Generally, their added details will be scandalous.

Samuel Johnson, the English playwright and lexicographer, was reputed to have a prodigious memory. A Mr Hector once recited eighteen verses of his poetry to Johnson. After a moment to gather his thoughts, Johnson recited them back.

Hector noted that only one line was different from the original – and it was improved!

If we must repeat what we hear, we might err the same way Samuel Johnson did, on the side of making the situation a better one!

Friday — October 22

I AM sure we have all heard the phrase "bury the hatchet" used for making peace. But, in a treaty between French colonists and the Mohawk people, the Mohawk chief used a different phrase.

"We have thrown the hatchet so high into the air and beyond the skies," he is recorded as saying, "that no arm on earth can reach to bring it down."

In other words, they had taken their weapons of war and entrusted them to the Great Spirit, or God. If only we could do the same with the things that divide us; give them to God so we might never take them up again ourselves.

Saturday — October 23

ST LAWRENCE CHURCH in Winchester is almost completely boxed in by town-centre shops and offices. But, still, it is a place of peace and prayer. On the day I crossed its threshold it was like a cool drink of water for my soul.

That was eight years ago. But, even now, I can remember that feeling. A place of peace is a wonderful thing to find, and one of the sweetest gifts to offer.

THEY looked like they needed help – and I was going to, but I was worried I might be being conned."

It's a real thing, and I am sure it has crossed each of our minds at one time or another.

And we do need to be sensible.

But when it is just a worry and it stops us helping, then we sacrifice kindness on the altar of fear.

What difference might it make to the world, our lives and the lives of those in difficult situations, if we grew more accustomed to sacrificing fear on the altar of kindness.

Monday — October 25

THE Hindu proverb read, "Help thy brother's boat across the sea. And, Lo! Thine own boat hath reached the shore."

At first, I thought it was a version of "You can't help someone else without helping yourself".

Then I realised. If the sea referred to is life, then the shore must be heaven. Could we ever get there without helping our brother or sister?

Which is why Jesus's greatest commandment may just have been, "Love one another!"

Tuesday — October 26

WHEN a person does a good deed when he or she didn't have to," the Jewish Talmud says, "God looks down and smiles and says, 'For this moment alone it was worth creating the world'."

It's a beautiful image, isn't it? But it does beg the question of what happens when someone chooses to do an unkind thing.

I like to imagine a sort of comic set of scales, with negative acts tipping the pointer one way, and positive acts tipping it the other.

Now, given that there are definitely people out there with a penchant for the negative, what shall we do to keep the scales tipped in the right direction?

Let's keep that smile on God's face!

Wednesday — October 27

IN "The Courtship Of Miles Standish", the poet Longfellow described Mr Standish this way: "Though he was rough, he was kindly".

If there is one thing I enjoy more than kindness, it's kindness from unexpected sources.

Like the man at the bus-stop. He wore old denims, had his hair in a top-knot and tattoos and piercings. Women standing there edged as far from him as they could. Then the bus arrived and he stood back. "Ladies first."

Kindliness often shines through a multitude of unlikely façades.

Thursday — October 28

THE French composer Claude Debussy once said, "We must agree that the beauty of a work of art will always remain a mystery. We can never be absolutely sure how it is made."

Those words came to my mind as my doggy friend and I were out walking through a field of red and gold leaves beneath a clear blue sky.

The individual parts of the composition were pretty, of course, but the combination of them filled my heart and soul in no easily explainable way.

In the end, I settled for mentally complimenting the Artist and appreciating His inexplicable mystery.

Friday — October 29

THERE'S a man who walks around Melbourne carrying a giant carrot. Why? Because It makes people smile.

He has tried other giant veg, but he reckons the home-made six-feet-tall carrot makes more people smile.

Crazy? Perhaps. Until you know he doesn't just wander aimlessly: he goes to protests, marches and potential flash-points to try to lighten the mood a little. Things tend not to tip into violence in the presence of a man hugging a big carrot.

Once I heard that, I wondered if we might not all get in on the giant veg act!

A **WORD** or two can tell you a lot.
I was on "playground supervision" duty while the parents took a break.

The grandson of a friend was playing with two children whose family I didn't know. Jake, the boy I didn't know, had invited Sam into his make-believe restaurant in the garden.

In a spirit of playful banter, Sam told him that McDonalds made much better burgers. Jake pretended to get irate and chased Sam out of the "restaurant" with a toy spatula.

Just as he did so, Evie, Jake's four-year-old sister, stepped into the midst of it all. Thinking the chase was for real, she shouted to her brother.

"Jake! Show him some grace!"

"OK, you can come back in," Jake told Sam.

They were four and six, and their parents had taught them about grace and undeserved second chances!

There and then, because of those few words, I fancied I knew a lot about them. I knew their upbringing had been loving, and I predicted only good things for their future.

Sunday — October 31

J **OHN WESLEY**, the founder of the Methodist movement, was a man of strong principle and, thus, sometimes difficult to get along with. He once had a falling-out with a Mr Bradford. When they could not agree on the matter Wesley suggested that they must part ways.

In the morning, after a night at an inn, the two met at breakfast in the same room.

Wesley asked Bradford if he had reconsidered. Would he ask Wesley's forgiveness, or must they actually never speak again?

Bradford refused. Wesley asked if he was sure. Bradford said he was.

Then Wesley said, "Well, my friend, I shall ask yours."

Bradford, deeply affected by this, gladly offered his forgiveness.

To be right is important. To stand on principle is important. To keep a friend, to Wesley, was the most important thing of all.

November

THE Pennsylvanian poet Bayard Taylor, a 19th-century Quaker, described November as a Puritan standing stern in the joyless fields, rebuking the lingering colour.

A bit harsh, perhaps. The Puritans had good intentions in wanting (among other things) people to derive their pleasure from God alone.

But, as so often happens, they went too far, and will be for ever remembered as having tried to outlaw pleasure.

Their influence can still be felt in places, but their time of ordering society's delight is long gone.

And much the same fate will befall the legacy of cold, bleak November – in one month and 24 days!

GEORGE and Susan have six grandchildren, all aged between four and six. The children don't often get to see each other and they are rarely all in the one place at the one time.

But they were all at George and Susan's house yesterday evening.

I asked if he had known what he was letting himself in for.

"Some of my very favourite childhood memories are from when my mum and dad took us to an auntie and uncle's house," he told me. "The grown-ups would party in the living-room and the kids would play in a bedroom.

"Sometimes there were six of us in a room with a bed, a wardrobe and a dressing-table . . . and we would play hide-and-seek!

"From the general hilarity we heard last night and how exhausted they were when they left, I'd say the same thing happened last night."

No electronic gadgetry was employed, and cousins never require batteries!

A cloud-filled sky full of promise.

Southern York County, Pennsylvania.

Wednesday — November 3

THE "man on a bench" was actually an art installation made of bronze alloy. That didn't stop the dog snuggling down on his lap. Despite the cold of the metal, the dog recognised the figure as a source of comfort and the lap as a place to be.

There are warmer places to seek affection. May we be such, or know of such in our lives.

Thursday — November 4

WHEN Robert Fulton was a boy, he had no interest in book-learning. Popular legend has him telling his teacher his head was too full of his own ideas to have any space for other people's.

He went on to create the world's first commercially viable paddle-steamer. A child's imagination is an under-utilised resource and it should never be discouraged.

Friday — November 5

ON Guy Fawkes Night we remember someone who tried to make a sudden, explosive difference to society.

The philosopher Socrates didn't expect people to come to him to hear his ideas. He took the ideas to the shipyards, the marketplaces, the village wells. Thus he had a huge influence on western culture.

The best way to make a difference is to set a better example. Let's try to blow people's minds by the way we live, rather than blow up their palaces.

Saturday — November 6

WHAT if I told you there was one thing that might guard the young from error, attend to the wants of the elderly, and provide those in their prime with the motivation to do good and noble deeds?

I can't take the credit for the idea, much as I would like to pretend I'm that smart. It came from the insights of the philosopher Aristotle. What did he say was good for all of those things? A friend!

IN the days when dance halls had mirror balls, the halls were often cut off from the outer world and dimly lit. A lamp that would never have lit the whole space was shone on to a mirror ball and the reflected rays of light would reach every corner of the hall.

God could surely light up every dark corner of the world.

Instead, he shines a fraction of his glory on each of us and entrusts us with reflecting it out into the dark corners of the world, or to those people who need it most.

How would you like to be a mirror ball?

NEVER put off till tomorrow what you can do today."
It is good advice, but sombre and perhaps a little depressing.

It suggests a heavy workload and a reluctance to see it through.

The words are credited to Philip Stanhope, 4th Earl of Chesterfield, and a renowned "man of letters".

Shortly before his most famous line come the words, "Know the true value of time; snatch, seize and enjoy every minute of it."

If we were more concerned with making the most of today, it could be that tomorrow's worries might find themselves already taken care of.

SYDNEY SMITH, the English writer and cleric, once replied to a friend asking how he was.

"I have gout, asthma and seven other maladies – but I am otherwise very well."

Perhaps he made a distinction between himself and his body.

His body might bear all sorts of aches and pains, but Sydney Smith might still be well and young in spirit.

We are more than our physical strengths and limitations. It's well worth remembering that when we are asked.

And at all other times, too!

Wednesday — November 10

I REALLY needed a long lie this morning. So, when someone knocked on the front door at seven a.m., I stumbled out of bed, muttering under my breath.

It was a delivery man. I almost asked him what he was doing knocking at that time, but I would have had to find him inside his waterproofs first. I looked beyond him into the rain and the dark.

I wondered what time he had started work that morning and how little he was being paid for it.

"Wonderful. Thank you very much!" I said, making a mental promise to try to be less grumpy and more appreciative for the rest of the day.

Thursday — November 11

WE were at the Royal Marines Memorial when Big Ben struck 11. I looked at the soldiers, dignitaries and families, wondering who and what they remembered.

Just then, a pizza delivery man on a motor-scooter passed by on the other side of the road. He turned, parked, took his helmet off and lowered his head in prayer. Then, without talking, he went about his work.

The echoes of war spread far and wide. If we can't always understand, may we at least offer grace.

Friday — November 12

YOUNG neighbours of ours are just back from a weekend in Prague.

"There was something magical about it," she said.

"Like the special feeling we found in Winchester," he added.

"We have been lucky in finding magical places," she agreed. "Like York. And the island of Arran . . . and Edinburgh."

I smiled and wondered how many "magical" places they would discover before they realised. As Walt Whitman, the great American writer, said, "Though we travel the world over to find the beautiful, we must carry it with us or we find it not."

Saturday — November 13

RENÉ DESCARTES, the French-Dutch philosopher, is probably best known for his statement, "I think, therefore I am." But a lesser-known maxim of his might help us all in times of conflict.

"When a man injures me, I strive to lift up my soul so high that his offence cannot reach me."

"I think" that is very good advice and "therefore I am" trying my very best to follow it.

Sunday — November 14

A FEW of my friends have taken to learning Gaelic. One told me of the different terms used for death.

A native Gaelic speaker might use the word *bas* to refer to the death of a farm animal or wild creature, but *caochail* for the death of a person.

Why? Well, the former term simply means "dead", but the latter means "changed" or "transformed".

On Remembrance Sunday, when we think of the war dead, let us not think of them as simply dead, sacrificed to the interests of their various governments.

Instead, let us think of them as transformed, existing happily in a time and place where there are no wars and peace reigns for ever.

Monday — November 15

THE autumn leaves fall quickly now,
They drift from every branch and bough;
With vibrant hues in every leaf,
They thickly carpet all beneath,
And even as the days grow dark
The sight provides a cheerful spark;
With colours bright as any flame
They put the finest rug to shame.
Despite chill mists and winds that bite,
November still can bring delight.

Maggie Ingall

Tuesday — November 16

IF there's one thing I really appreciate on these cold, windy days, it's a hot drink. You can't beat a good cup of tea.

I'm not alone in thinking that, and no less a person than Prime Minister William Gladstone agreed.

I believe it was him who said the following:

"If you are cold, tea will warm you;
If you are too heated, it will cool you.
If you are depressed, it will cheer you.
If you are excited, it will calm you."

Wednesday — November 17

IMAGINE, if you will, a man or woman walking along and finding a friend buried up to their neck in troubles.

Being a good sort, of course they dig them out.

But they know that if they shovel the dirt back into the hole, it will still be quite a bit short of the surface.

After all, their friend is no longer in there. It might be a hazard to others.

So, they take all their own troubles and tip them into the hole. Then they top it off with dirt.

The ground is now flat and level and two people are better off, because one person stopped to help.

Thursday — November 18

WHAT do you think of as consolation? A second-best prize? Trying to make someone who is sad feel better?

The "con" in consolation means "to be with". The second part of the word refers to "the lonely".

So consolation means being with the lonely.

At times of loss, there can often be no second-best prize, and making anything better can seem impossible.

But we can be with them, saying nothing if need be, just being with the lonely.

Friday — November 19

SHE fell asleep on the bus between the airport and the railway station. Her suitcase had wheels on it and the bus went round bends, but the suitcase never moved. The man behind her had his foot against it and at times reached forward to stop it toppling over.

She left the bus not knowing how she'd been looked after.

How many times a day do we benefit from the actions of good Samaritans (or angels in disguise), and never know a thing about it?

Saturday — November 20

ANNE BRONTË was the youngest of the sisters. Unlike Charlotte and Emily, her writing was towards the realistic rather than the romantic. But one doesn't necessarily exclude the other.

"Because the road is rough and long, shall we despise the skylark's song that cheers the wanderer's way?" she wrote.

Sunday — November 21

A SWEET PEA competition was run by the "Daily Mail" in 1911. The minister of Sprouston's flowers were chosen out of 38,000 entrants. He did a lot of good with the prize money.

It's a wonderful story. But what impressed me most was that the "Daily Mail" thought a bunch of sweet peas worth a prize of £1,000.

A ridiculous amount? Or a proper evaluation for some of God's prettiest work?

Monday — November 22

EVERY saint and every sinner affects those whom he will never see, because his words and deeds stamp themselves upon the soft clay of human nature everywhere," Rabbi Joshua L. Liebman wrote.

Think about those people you know. If we believed that our words or actions left an indelible mark on them, would we be happy with that? Or would we feel compelled to change, at least a little?

Of course, the more positive that impact became, the better we would be. So both sides win.

Tuesday — November 23

SIR ROBERT SHIRLEY was a 16th- and 17th-century soldier and adventurer. He led a life of privilege but worked hard for it and frequently risked everything.

He trained Persian armies and fought against the Ottoman Empire, and his travels in Europe resulted in him being made a Knight of the Holy Roman Empire.

But what interested me most were the words engraved over the door of the church founded in Leicestershire by Shirley.

". . . whose singular praise it is to have done the best things in ye worst times And hoped them in the most calamitous."

Wednesday — November 24

MARY KNOWLES, a campaigning Quaker poet, lived in England in the second half of the 18th century.

As strange as it seems now, one of her battles was for the right of women to choose their own husbands.

She also penned this simplistic but charming advice.

"Eat little at night, open your windows, drive out often and look for the good in things and in people . . . and you will no longer be sad, bored, or ill."

I cannot vouch for the curative properties of the things she suggested, but they do sound like an excellent way to live a life, all the same.

Thursday — November 25

*N*OVEMBER *is a time for touching hearts*
For sharing thoughts and showing that we care,
For reaching out with love and understanding,
With prayers for peace for people everywhere.
November days are sometimes grey and gloomy,
But seek for brightness, let that be your goal,
And we have love, enduring and eternal.
Hold on to love to warm your heart and soul.

Iris Hesselden

Let the outside into your life and you will open your heart.

Friday — November 26

IN Victor Hugo's *"Les Misérables"*, Laigle is one of the band of young idealistic revolutionaries.

"My coat and I live comfortably together. It has assumed all my wrinkles, does not hurt me anywhere, has moulded itself on my deformities, and is complacent in all my movements, and I only feel its presence because it keeps me warm."

Doesn't that sound like a description of an ideal friend?

Saturday — November 27

A LITTLE girl apologised for disturbing me at my work and asked if I could braid her toy pony's mane. As busy as I undoubtedly was, I stopped and said, "Of course."

It reminded me of Lord Halifax who, in the 1940s, was Ambassador to the United States. The Ambassador's Office was aware of the importance of being impartial in American politics.

Travelling on a sleeper train, he struck up a friendship with a little boy. The boy wanted to give the Ambassador something that meant a lot to him. A "MacArthur For President" badge!

Lord Halifax wore it for the rest of the journey, hiding it with a hankie and removing the hankie whenever the little boy was around. That way, he stayed as true as he could to both of his trusts.

Sunday — November 28

THE postcard of a Scottish village scene must be 120 years old. The roads are empty but for a horse, cart and children. The girls wear bonnets, the boys have polished shoes. I would guess the photo was taken on a Sunday, the children on their way to Sunday School.

How rough their lives were the rest of the week, I can only guess, but the Sabbath then was a day of rest.

Across the bottom of the postcard were inked some appropriate words, written by William C. Bryant, the American poet and long-time editor of the "New York Evening Post": *There is a day of sunny rest for every dark and troubled night.*"

If you have troubled nights, may you find those sunny days. And plenty of them.

THOSE of a certain generation will remember grocers wearing them, or butchers, bakers, cobblers – or any number of tradespeople.

But our fondest memories of them will be associated with our mothers and grandmothers as they went about their household chores.

We might have hidden behind them, or had our faces wiped with them, or simply held on to them.

We don't see them so much these days.

I am, of course, talking about aprons.

The one thing almost all of the apron-wearers had in common is summed up by a line in the book of 1 Peter, which can be translated as "putting on the apron of humility to be of service to others".

Aprons might not be so much in fashion these days. But I hope humility and service always will be.

I HAVE heard of it being done in big ways and small ways. The big version is probably well described in the story of a Kilmarnock minister, leaving his manse after 40 years of service to his parish.

Once the door closed behind them, the minister and his wife turned to face it.

Then they kneeled on the stone step, closed their eyes and thanked God for the house and for all it had been to them and the family who had grown up there.

The small version came about when the shaft of Harry's garden fork began to split.

He laid it atop a bonfire, planning to reclaim the metal after the wood turned to ashes.

"You were a good help in a lot of hard work. People enjoyed the end results," he muttered, thinking no-one could hear him.

We do live in a disposable culture these days (although, hopefully, that is changing), but let's not get into the habit of disposing of anything without properly appreciating all the good it did first.

Charles Dickens's "A Christmas Carol" continues to inspire.

Christmas lights on Oxford Street, London.

December

JUST recently, I have been complaining to the Lady Of The House that doing so many things for so many people wasn't leaving me enough time for my "proper" work.

Then I went to see a production of "A Christmas Carol". Jacob Marley was wrapped in iron chains made from ledgers, receipts and cash boxes because he had thought these things were his business.

"Mankind was my business. The common welfare was my business; charity, mercy, forbearance and benevolence were all my business. The dealings of my trade were but a drop of water in the comprehensive ocean of my business!"

Something got in my eye about then. After I wiped it away, I thought maybe I should complain a little less – and get on with my proper business.

JONATHAN had been on a tour of a Naval construction yard. He's an ex-Navy man, but he's used to seeing these ships from the inside, and already built.

He was fascinated by the techniques used, the sizes on the machinery and so on, but one fact impressed him more than any other. The guide had informed them the amount of paperwork it takes to get an aircraft carrier built would sink an aircraft carrier!

"Is it true?" I asked him

"I'm going to assume it is," he replied, "and not just because the guide said so, but because I have seen people struggle to stay afloat under the weight of everything it took to get them to a particular point in their lives.

"Remember, though," he added, "the aircraft carrier floats because it doesn't carry all that unnecessary weight."

And we don't need to, either. Float on!

Friday — December 3

HOPE BOURNE, who lived most of her life on Exmoor, described standing in the sunshine one morning among the ash trees, the woodruff, the brambles, the St John's wort, the gorse . . .

"So much to delight the passer-by," she wrote in "A Moorland Year". "So much beauty for no cost at all."

Do you have somewhere like that near you? Then don't forget to appreciate it.

Not everyone has Exmoor on their doorstep. Some live in built-up areas. But even there the sun still shines, and nature will find a way.

It will be all the more beautiful because of its scarcity and its tenacity.

Saturday — December 4

I WAS visiting Warren for a cuppa and a catch-up. He has limited movement and normally he takes a pride in bringing the tea tray from the kitchen to the living-room.

This time he invited me into the kitchen to see his pot plant. I did not have high expectations as I walked through.

The cactus on his kitchen window-sill, between the washing-up liquid and a jar he keeps screws in, had turned towards the weak, wintery sun.

Its yellow petals, which seemed gold in the sunlight, were reaching back, exposing a delicate, narrow funnel from which a scarlet stamen protruded.

We both looked at them. I saw pretty flowers. He saw "golden dragons in flight".

I looked again. The back-turned petals did look like wings. The stamen did look like a breath of fire.

From then on I saw nothing but a flight of golden dragons whenever I looked at the flower pot.

And, surprisingly, I did appreciate the cactus more for Warren's notion.

We sometimes laugh at those among us who have more fantastical notions of what the world is like, or what it is all about.

I prefer to think it really is that wonderful, and people like Warren are our gentle, wonderful reminders.

S HE came to Sunday services and the weekday groups. The part of church she liked the least was the weekly sermon. I asked her why.

"Oh, he reads from the Bible, but most of his stories are about him. He's just too full of himself."

She didn't know the minister well enough to understand he is a humble man. What he was doing was sharing his own experience of the ups and downs, the pitfalls and hilltop moments, of a faith lived.

And faith should be lived, not just read!

Monday — December 6

E LSA'S mother used to take her and her sister for drives to various beauty spots when they were little. Now Elsa does the same with her grandchildren.

When they arrive, she always tells them her mum took her there.

"Do you think it means anything to them?" I asked, meeting them one day.

"Consciously? No. But every child, subconsciously, wants to be safe and to be loved.

"When I take them to these places I let them know that someone who loved someone they love came here first; someone who would also have loved them.

"And it has a very similar effect on me."

Tuesday — December 7

T HE advice in the fortune cookie read *Be happy. A reason will come along.*

"Reasons to be happy will come along eventually. Might as well be happy in between them," one of my friends said.

"I suppose if you are already happy, you might be more receptive to reasons for being like that," another suggested.

A third offered that knowing something worth being happy about will eventually come along is a decent reason to actually be happy.

I agreed with all three and mentally summed them up in one piece of advice. It was, "Be happy. A reason will come along."

"God rest ye, merry gentlemen . . ."

WE tell the Christmas story
Through carols that we sing,
The story of a baby boy
Born humbly, to be King.

These carols, so familiar,
Bring comfort and good cheer,
As we recall that winter's night
We celebrate each year.

And whether in a church we sing
Or round a Christmas tree,
The hopes we share remain the same
For peace and harmony.

John Darley

Thursday — December 9

I CAME across an old Arabic proverb. It said something like, "These days you complain about, one day you will cry for."

I hear a lot of people talking about "the good old days". I remember people doing that in the good old days!

Some of my favourite times when I was a child were spent with my grandmother.

The high-backed chair she sat in beside the fireplace also guarded the cupboard that housed the electricity meter.

It was my delight to be allowed to put a shilling in the meter, turn the handle and bring the lights back on.

Ah, the good old days!

The fact of the matter is that, having grown up on a farm with no electricity at all, those were very modern days for my grandmother.

And she would tell me stories of her own childhood and finding her way to bed with a candle.

Every new day will eventually be an old day. Fill the new ones with love and we will never need to cry for old.

Friday — December 10

I DO like learning new words. Recently, I discovered *Hyggelig*. It is a Scandinavian greeting, meaning "nice to see you".

But it also describes the enjoyment of simple, cosy and comfortable things.

When better, in these bleak winter days, than to settle down with a blanket, a book, a nice coffee, or perhaps a chocolate or two?

And, if you are that way inclined, you might double the pleasure by sharing it with someone it would be nice to see.

Each version of the word will brighten up a chilly day. The combination of the two would surely be delightful.

Saturday — December 11

IT had been a trying time for my friend, but it seemed to bring out the philosopher in her.

"I worried and worried," she told me, "and it made no difference to how things turned out. I did something wrong and I beat myself up about it for decades – but the wrong thing stayed a wrong thing.

"I woke up on a nothing-much sort of day. I gave sincere thanks for it, and it was instantly a better day!"

Regret won't change the past. Worry can't predict the future. But appreciation can make anything special.

It would surely benefit us to think about how much "head space" we give each of them.

Sunday — December 12

JALALUDDIN RUMI was a Sufi mystic. His poetry has become loved around the world.

His insights transcend denominations, reaching for a higher truth.

"On a day when the wind is perfect, the sail just needs to open and the love begins. Today is such a day."

The last line is important because every day is such a day.

If, at any time on our voyage through life, we care to open our sail – that is, be receptive – then love will fill us.

Monday — December 13

PLACED the star on top of the tree (straightening it under my sweetheart's direction).

The Lady Of The House had bedecked it with tinsel, lights and baubles, many of which were souvenirs of places we had been and people we loved.

"We have so much." She sighed. "My friend, Gracie, told me how some people in the Philippines make Christmas trees out of branches and sprinkle grated soap over them to make them look snow-covered."

"Would you like that?" I asked.

"Well . . ." She thought. "It would remind us to be humble."

Tuesday — December 14

NEIL MUNRO was a Scottish journalist and the author of the "Vital Spark" novels. In his novel "The Shoes Of Fortune" his character, Father Hamilton, dies after saving a child.

As a friend sits by his side weeping, he sums up all the wisdom he has gained in life.

"Be good, be simple, be kind. 'Tis all I know. Fifty years to learn it, and I might have found it at my mother's lap!"

How often do we lose sight of the most profound truths by looking for something more complex, less simple?

We all might learn things worth learning, sitting at the feet of mothers.

Wednesday — December 15

IF I were to say it, or if you did, there would be people who dismissed it as nonsense. Which, in itself, proves the saying.

Blaise Pascal was a man who knew a thing or two. He was a French mathematician, physicist, inventor and theologian.

"We conceal it from ourselves in vain – we must always love something."

We either suffer from the lack of it (denying that it matters), or we love. It is that essential to our being. I would prefer to love!

Thursday — December 16

DO enjoy this "adjusted" Christmas "to-do" list. Here is the original: *To do: Buy presents. Wrap gifts. Send gifts. Shop for food.*

The adjusted version read, *To do: Be present. Wrap someone in a hug. Share food with someone who wouldn't normally have a Christmas dinner.*

The first is a list of what some think is necessary and important. The second is much closer to the spirit of the season.

Friday — December 17

IN the book "The Friendly Year", published in 1940, H.L. Gee talks of an encounter with a ploughman.

In passing, he describes how, after their chat, the man put his hat on his head "and, with a nod, turned back, took up the handles, called softly to the horses and went striding across the faithful, patient soil, his eyes fixed on some distant landmark to help him plough a straight furrow."

A distant landmark? It might be something different for different people, but there is no doubting its importance when it comes to keeping us on track. I know what mine is.

Saturday — December 18

HAVE you heard anyone carolling in your neighbourhood yet? Have you been out carolling yet?

Christmas carols – the best of them, done as they ought to be – have a transcendent feeling to them. They take us to a place beyond the norm: a special, joyous place.

Writing them is an art form, and I thought of those "artists" when I read these words in the novel "Donal Grant" by the Scottish writer and preacher George MacDonald: "One has mastery who makes the joy the last in every song."

Of course, that doesn't just apply to song-writers, it also applies to those singers who put their heart and soul into their performance.

Joy to the last. I cannot think of a better way to write, to sing or to live!

To do list

1.
2.
3.
4.
5.

What will be on your
Christmas list?

Sunday — December 19

BECAUSE someone decided I was good at talking to children (or perhaps they thought I was childish), I get to be part of the Christmas church services for the local primary schools.

The church gets moved around a little for these events and the beautiful Nativity scene had been shifted to the side aisles. But this was where the schoolchildren filed in.

From my temporary vantage point on the balcony, I saw a group of children bump the table it stood on, rolling the baby Jesus out and on to the floor. Others filed past. But one little lad picked him up, laid him in the manger, then stroked his head reassuringly before moving on.

I felt humbled by the small gesture, and the reminder that, no matter how commercialised the time of year becomes, no matter what is or isn't politically correct, it is each of us – in our hearts – who puts Christ in Christmas.

Monday — December 20

FOUR-YEAR-OLD Evie and six-year-old Elias just went to their first-ever pantomime. They are American and the tradition isn't so big there.

They were visiting Gran Julie in Scotland, so she took them along.

"Their eyes were wide with amazement the whole time," she told me.

"Panto can be quite a spectacle," I agreed.

But Gran Julie explained that there was more to it than that. A local drama group had provided the entertainment. The church provided the hall. Admission was free.

Santa was a volunteer. Local charities gave out selection boxes and donated gifts. A local ice-cream parlour gave everyone free tubs of ice-cream. The hall was full to bursting.

"What my grandchildren saw," Julie added, "was a deprived community pulling together for its children. The entertainment was wonderful. There was more to it than that, of course, but children don't need to know about that.

"They just need to know that Cinderella, the Prince and Buttons came together to take on the bad guys – and that good won!

THE days before Christmas are, traditionally, very busy times for airlines and bus companies. So many people feel the need to get to the people they love for the holidays.

One of the funniest and most heart-tugging films made on the subject has to be "Planes, Trains And Automobiles".

In it, John Candy and Steve Martin get stuck with each other in a chaotic attempt to get home for Christmas.

It turns out that home is a different thing for each of them.

Hal Borland wrote many books and articles on the "great outdoors", so he would surely have known the joy of coming home.

"To know after absence the familiar street and road and village and house is to know again the satisfaction of home."

Walking the old street to the familiar door is part of the idea of home. But the essence of it is the people who wait beyond the door. And the essence of our relationship with them is, or should be, love.

Love is our natural home. Perhaps we feel the need for it more at Christmas, but it is a truth for the rest of the year as well. Every year.

Be with someone in passionate love, or filial love, or spiritual love, and you will already be home.

Wednesday — December 22

FROM this point on, the days start getting longer. The worst weather of the year still lies ahead, but at least we shall "suffer" it in more and more sunlight.

There will be bleak and miserable days ahead, but there will be crisp and fresh days as well, and we might see them if we don't always hide away. We might play the game of trying to spot the first signs of winter as soon as possible.

John Burroughs, who lived around the turn of the 20th century, was a nature essayist. He thought every part of the year was worth paying attention to.

He who marvels at the beauty of the world in summer will find equal cause for wonder and admiration in winter.

Find some stout shoes, a warm coat and a walking companion. Then put that extra daylight to good use!

Thursday — December 23

PETER is a fire-fighter at an airport. Because planes come in all through the holidays, it means that some of them have to be on duty over Christmas.

"Sometimes it can be a miserable shift," he told me. "It gets a little more interesting when it snows because we have to help keep the runways clear.

"We had just done a stint on that and we were cold and wet, while it seemed the rest of the world was celebrating. And then . . . someone picked up a snowball! Pretty soon it became the most fun I'd had in a long time!"

The Christmas spirit will get you one way or another. Let's remember those working for our safety and comfort during the holiday, and do our bit to help the Christmas spirit find them.

Friday — December 24

CHRISTMAS Eve! Could it be possible that I like it more than the big day itself? All the focus is on the 25th and the build-up to it.

But once the shops are shut on the 24th, once all the journeys are made and everyone is where they are supposed to be, once the furniture is rearranged and the last gift has been placed under the tree, there is a brief time for doing nothing.

In the beginning of that "nothing" time our minds are set free from preparations. We have time to think of others, those no longer with us and those we might still be able to include in the next day's celebrations. What we are doing all this for.

Then there is only the waiting left, and the trusting.

On a clear night, I like to step into the back garden, not to pray, or to say or think anything, just to be at one with Creation and know that I am a part of God's plan. As are each and every one of us.

In the time when everything else is either done or waiting to happen, in that space we find God and faith.

"Silent Night" is more than just a carol. It's a necessary communion, a recharging of the soul from which we take peace and love into the business of the party season and the year ahead.

May we all find a little of that precious silent night; that beautiful holy night.

Saturday — December 25

THERE is a piece of popular wisdom "Dance like no-one is watching," it begins.

Well, someone updated it for Christmas. Now it suggests we, "Dance like Frosty the Snowman, shine like Rudolph the Red-Nosed Reindeer, give like Santa and love like Jesus!"

A little frivolous. And I'm not altogether sure how well snowmen dance.

But, if we were to take them seriously – especially the last one – I have absolutely no doubt we would have a joyous Noel!

Sunday — December 26

DID you have your birthday on Christmas Day? Do you know someone who did?

It can be a frustrating occurrence for children, especially when some insensitive adults give them only one gift for their birthday and their Christmas.

Reassuring them that Jesus would have had the same problem probably isn't much of a comfort.

Thankfully, there are still adults out there who understand how children feel. One such was Robert Louis Stevenson.

In the year "Treasure Island" was published, the Scottish author received a letter from twelve-year-old Annie Ide, a fan and the daughter of a friend.

In it, after praising his books, she complained about her birthday falling on Christmas Day.

Most people would have sympathised. Stevenson went further than that.

He declared the matter "out of all reason" and therefore "out of all justice". Having reached an age where he no longer had any use for his own birthday (in November), he officially transferred it to her.

He went so far as having his request drawn up as a legal document and even had a lord witness it.

Now, I am not suggesting giving away perfectly good birthdays, but if you have one you no longer use lying around, perhaps you might know a youngster who would appreciate it.

Monday — December 27

THAT'S another year almost done. Hopefully, it had its fair share of golden moments and new friendships. Inevitably, though, it will have had cross words and unhappy partings.

In the year to come we can hope for a similar crop of happiness. But what to do with those upsets? They might be in the past, but they still cast a shadow.

The American pastor Harry Emerson Fosdick wrote, "Bitterness imprisons life, love releases it."

Don't chain next year in last year's problems, no matter whose fault they were. Set it – and yourself – free, in forgiveness and love.

Tuesday — December 28

READ the phrase in an old book and a memory responded, causing me to think how times had changed.

Long ago, if someone had provided you with hospitality, etiquette demanded you send them a "bread and butter letter".

It might have been called that because it was generally a work-a-day note, a short and simple thank-you. Or it might literally have been because, sometimes, bread and butter (and a bed) was all the hosts had to offer.

Now that many of us have more than the basics in our own home, have we lost our appreciation of the littler things?

I do hope not. Bread and butter when you are hungry really is something to be thankful for.

Wednesday — December 29

IN a season of gifts, here is a little reminder for the rest of the year. Kahlil Gibran was a Lebanese-American poet and philosopher.

"It is well to give when asked, but it is better to give when unasked, through understanding."

A gift that you asked for, or that you get for a Christmas or a birthday, can be a delight. But to know that someone saw your unexpressed pain or need, thought of a help for it and gave it to you – that's priceless!

WHEN making a start on this journey,
The journey we all know as life,
A magic, meandering mystery tour
Where pleasures and perils are rife.
We may not know what the future holds,
From one precious hour to the next;
The pages in the book are blank –
It's us who write the text.
But one thing is certain and never in doubt
No matter the length of the play,
Though some may go steerage and others first class
The tickets are always one-way.
And as the clock cannot be stopped
Or even turned back to the start,
Each second marks a compass point
Upon our lifetime's chart.
And when, at last, the dots are joined,
The pathway in plain sight,
Let's hope our every step has left
A residue of light.

Tricia Sturgeon

ICELANDERS are famously fond of reading. Given the long, dark winters, putting your feet up with a good book seems a very nice idea. So many books are sold between September and Christmas they have a name for it – the *Jolabokaflod* or the Christmas Book Flood.

It's a tradition that seems to have its roots in the harsh times of World War II, when paper was one of the few things not rationed.

But what do books have to do with New Year's Eve? For that we go to Edith Lovejoy Pierce, an English poet born in 1904. She referred to the year ahead as a book.

"We will open the book. Its pages are blank. We are going to put words on them ourselves. The book is called Opportunity and its first chapter is New Year's Day."

May your "book" be a wonderful one.

Is there anything better than cosying up with a good book?